Camera
Terms and Concepts

David E. Elkins

City of **Westminster College**
Paddington **Learning Centre**
25 Paddington **Green**
London **W2 1NB**

Focal Press
Boston   London

Focal Handbooks

Steven E. Browne	*Film ◆ Video Terms and Concepts*
David E. Elkins	*Camera Terms and Concepts*
Arthur Schneider	*Electronic Post-Production Terms and Concepts*

Focal Press is an imprint of Butterworth–Heinemann.

Copyright © 1993 by Butterworth–Heinemann, a division of Reed Publishing (USA) Inc. All rights reserved.

Library of Congress Cataloging-in-Publication Data
Elkins, David E.
    Camera terms and concepts / by David E. Elkins.
        p.   cm.—(Focal handbooks)
      ISBN 0-240-80150-4 (pbk)
      1. Motion picture cameras—Dictionaries. 2. Cinematography—
Dictionaries. I. Title. II. Title: Camera terms and concepts.
    III. Series.
    TR880.E44   1993   92-24981
    778.5'3—dc20

British Library Cataloguing-in-Publication Data
A catalogue record for this book is available from the British Library.

Butterworth–Heinemann
80 Montvale Avenue
Stoneham, MA 02180

10 9 8 7 6 5 4 3 2 1

Printed in the United States of America

Preface

In the motion picture industry and, specifically, the camera department, there are a variety of terms and specialized names of equipment with which you must become familiar. With this dictionary, I hope that you will find it easier to learn the day-to-day terminology used on the film set. There are many different terms and phrases used for the same thing, and I have tried to include the most common ones here. No book can be 100 percent complete, so please forgive me if there are any terms you would like to know that I have not included.

This book is for beginners, students, and anybody who wishes to learn the terms and phrases used by the camera crew and other technicians on a production. Instead of offering just the basic definition of certain terms, I have expanded many of the definitions so that they would be more easily understood. Included are many illustrations and photographs that should further help you to understand the definitions.

Acknowledgments

Many people and corporations contributed to the preparation of this book. Without the many photos and illustrations that I received, this book would not be complete. I would like to thank the following people and companies for their help and support: Arriflex Corporation; Chapman/Leonard Studio Equipment; G & M Power Products, Inc.; J.L. Fisher, Inc., Minolta Corporation; O'Connor Camera Support Systems; Panavision, Inc.; Panther Corporation of America; Sachtler Corporation; Camera Platforms International, Inc.; and Spectra Cine, Inc. Special thanks to Steve Chamberlain at Arriflex and Frank Kay at Panavision for taking time out of their busy schedules to speak with me and provide many photos and illustrations. Thanks to my many coworkers who offered suggestions and definitions for various terms and to Focal Press and Sharon Falter for asking me to write this book.

Finally, and most importantly, thanks to my family and friends who have understood and offered support through the years.

Aaton   Trade name of professional 16mm and 35mm cameras manufactured by Aaton Corporation. The commonly used Aaton cameras are the *XTR* for 16mm and the *Aaton 35* for 35mm.

Abby Singer shot   During production, the next-to-the-last shot of the day. According to Mr. Abby Singer, the term was first used during the mid-1950s while he was an assistant director at Universal Studios. In order to keep ahead of things, he would always inform the crew that they would shoot the current shot plus one more shot before moving to a different area of the studio, either a different stage or the back lot. Through the years, the term was used by other assistant directors, until today when it is always used to indicate the next-to-the-last shot of the day.

above the line   The costs incurred on a production before actual shooting begins. It also refers to the creative, nontechnical personnel on a production. Above-the-line costs usually include story and screenplay rights and wages for the producer, director, screenwriter, and cast members. Above-the-line personnel usually include producers, writers, directors, and actors.

A.C.   See *camera assistant.*

academy aperture (academy format)   The image size of a frame of 35mm motion picture film. At the time that 35mm film was invented, the picture area was 1 1/3 times as wide as it was high, so the ratio of the width to the height is written 1.33:1. Academy format is still used for almost all of the TV series and TV movies seen today, but feature films use the standard 1.85:1 format (Figure A.1).

Academy Awards   Also called **Oscars**. Annual awards presented by the Academy of Motion Picture Arts and Sciences to performers and technicians in the motion picture industry. First presented in 1927, the awards recognize artistic and technical excellence in various catego-

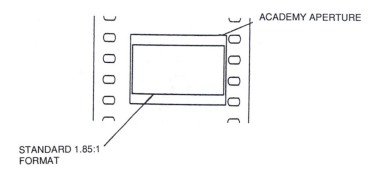

Figure A.1   Enlarged view of 35mm film frame showing academy aperture and 1.85:1 format. (Not drawn to scale.) (Reprinted from *The ARRI 35 Book*, with permission of the Arriflex Corporation. Diagrams courtesy of Clairmont Camera.)

ries. Academy members in each branch of the film industry select up to five nominees for their particular craft (actors select actors, directors select directors, etc.). All the members of that branch then choose the winner in their category by a secret ballot. The entire Academy membership then votes for the winner in the Best Picture category.

Academy of Motion Picture Arts and Sciences   An honorary organization comprised of actors and technicians in the film industry. It was founded in 1927 to promote a variety of objectives in the film industry. Membership is by invitation only. The members of the Academy are responsible for nominating and choosing the yearly winners of the Academy Awards. See also *Academy Awards*.

acetate base   A film base made of a slow-burning chemical substance that is much more durable than the older nitrate film base, which was highly flammable. Film that is coated onto an acetate base is sometimes referred to as *safety film*.

"Action"   What the director calls out to indicate that the actors should begin performing or that the action in the scene should begin. The director does not call this out until both the camera and sound recorder are running at sync speed, and the second camera assistant has clapped the slate.

actor/actress   A person who performs in any type of play, film, television show, and so forth. Most of the performers in films and television are union members. There are three guilds or unions that govern the various actors and actresses. They are the Screen Actors Guild (SAG), the American Federation of Television and Radio Artists (AFTRA), and Actors Equity.

AD   See *assistant director.*

aerial shot   Any filmed shot that is done from a very high angle, usually from a plane or helicopter.

Agfa   Trade name for a brand of professional motion picture film stock.

AFI   See *American Film Institute.*

AFTRA   See *American Federation of Television and Radio Artists.*

AKS   A slang term used to refer to an assortment of equipment, tools, and accessories. Any case that contains many different pieces of equipment or accessories is called an AKS case. It can be literally translated to mean "All Kinds of Stuff."

ambience (ambient sound)   The normal sound that occurs in a particular scene or location; for example, traffic noise, the chirping of birds, or the chatter of people gathered in one area. See also *room tone.*

American Cinematographer   A trade magazine that is published monthly by the American Society of Cinematographers. Each issue contains many articles about recent filmed productions as well as a featured article dealing with an older, sometimes classic, film. It also contains information about new technology and equipment.

American Cinematographer's Manual   See *ASC Manual.*

American Federation of Television and Radio Artists   The union to which actors and actresses who work in television and radio belong.

American Film Institute (AFI)   A private, nonprofit organization that was created to preserve the heritage of film and to advance the art of film. It is based in Washington, D.C., and has a branch in Los Angeles, California. The Los Angeles campus of AFI is the location of The Center for Advanced Studies, a prominent film school, and the Louis B. Mayer Library, which contains numerous books and screenplays. Each year the AFI presents a Lifetime Achievement award to a member of the film industry who has made significant contributions to the film industry. Some of the winners of this award include actors Henry Fonda, James Stewart, Bette Davis, and Lillian Gish and directors Alfred Hitchcock, David Lean, Orson Welles, and Frank Capra.

American Society of Cinematographers (ASC)   An honorary organization of cinematographers. It was founded in 1919 to advance the art of cinematography. Membership is extended by invitation only to qualified directors of photography. In the screen credits of a production, the initials *ASC* usually follow the name of the director of photography. The ASC also publishes many books and the magazine *American Cinematographer.* The British and Canadian counterparts to the ASC are the British Society of Cinematographers (BSC) and the Canadian Society of Cinematographers (CSC); respectively.

American Standards Association (ASA)   The organization that sets the requirements for rating a film stock's sensitivity to light. See also *ASA number.*

anamorphic lens   A film lens that allows the filming of wide-screen format when using standard 35mm film. It produces an image that is squeezed, or compressed, to fit the film frame. The developed print of the film is projected through a special projector using a similar type lens that unsqueezes the image and makes it appear normal on the screen.

angle, camera   See *camera angle.*

angle of view   Also called **field of view**. The angle covered by the camera lens.

answer print   The first print of the film that is done by the lab after editing has been completed and that contains the final sound and picture. It will be used to determine what the final release print to the theaters will look like and may require some color correction before being made into the final release print. See also *release print.*

antihalation backing   One of the three main components that make up any piece of film stock. It is the dark coating on the back of the unexposed film stock (Figure A.2), which prevents light from passing through the film, striking the back of the aperture, and then going back through the film causing a flare or fogging of the film image.

aperture (camera)   The opening in the film gate or aperture plate that determines the precise area of exposure of the frame of film. It determines the frame size by allowing light to only strike a portion of the frame and by preventing light from striking the edges of the film. During the brief time of exposure, the film is held in place in the gate by the registration pin, and light passes through the aperture striking the film and creating the image.

Figure A.2   Enlarged view of film stock showing the three components. (Not drawn to scale.)

aperture (lens)   The opening in the lens that is formed by an adjustable iris. It controls the amount of light that strikes the film.

aperture plate   The metal plate, within the camera, that has the aperture, or opening that determines the size of the exposed frame of film. See also *aperture (camera)*.

apple box   A wooden box, available in various sizes, that is used to raise the height of objects or actors in a scene. The standard sizes of apple boxes are full, half, quarter, and eighth. An eighth apple box is sometimes called a *pancake*.

Arri   See *Arriflex*.

Arriflex (Arri)   The trade name for a brand of 16mm and 35mm motion picture camera manufactured by the Arriflex Corporation in Germany. The company was founded in 1917 and is named for the two founders of the company, August Arnold and Robert Richter. Some of the most commonly used Arriflex cameras include the BL4s (Figure A.3), the 535 (Figures A.4, A.5), and the 35-3 (Figure A.6) for 35mm and the SRII (Figure A.7) for 35mm.

Arriglow   Trade name used by Arriflex Corporation for the illuminated frame lines of the ground glass. When filming in low-light situations, the Arriglow switch may be turned on so that the frame lines are illuminated making it easier for the camera operator to frame the shot.

artificial light   Any light that is created from a manmade source, such as spotlights, floodlights, softlights, and so on. It is the opposite of *natural light*. When using artificial light with certain film stocks, specifically daylight balanced film, an exposure compensation must be made in order for the film image to look natural.

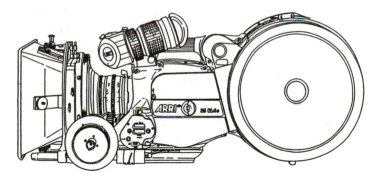

Figure A.3   Arriflex 35 BL4 camera. (Reprinted from *The ARRI Book*, with permission of the Arriflex Corporation.)

Figure A.4   Arriflex 535 camera—left side. (Photo courtesy of the Arriflex Corporation.)

Figure A.5   Arriflex 535 camera—reft side. (Photo courtesy of the Arriflex Corporation.)

Figure A.6   Arriflex 35-3 camera. (Photo courtesy of the Arriflex Corporation.)

ASA   See *American Standards Association.*

ASA number   A number assigned to each film stock to indicate the speed of the film, or the sensitivity of the film to light. The higher the number, the more sensitive the film is to light. A film stock with a low ASA number may be referred to as slow film, and one with a high ASA number may be referred to as fast film or high-speed film. The ASA number is used by the director of photography to determine the exposure. The ASA number may also be referred to as the *EI,* or *exposure index.* See also *DIN number; exposure index.*

Figure A.7   Arriflex 16SRII camera. (Photo courtesy of the Arriflex Corporation.)

ASC   See *American Society of Cinematographers.*

ASC Manual   A technical manual that is published by the American Society of Cinematographers. It contains useful information needed by directors of photography and camera assistants during shooting. This includes information on cameras, lighting, filters, depth of field, exposure compensation, film-speed tables, and so on. Most DPs and camera assistants keep a copy of this book in their meter case or ditty bag.

aspect ratio   Also called **format**. The relationship between the width of the frame and the height of the frame. It is always referred to as a ratio of width to height. For television and 16mm films, the standard aspect ratio is 1.33:1; for standard theatrical 35mm feature films, it is 1.85:1; and for anamorphic 35mm films, it is 2.35:1.

Aspheron   A 16mm lens attachment that is designed for the 9.5mm and the 12mm Zeiss prime lenses. It is used to increase the angle of view of these wide-angle lenses.

assistant cameraman   See *camera assistant.*

assistant director (AD)   A member of the crew who works closely with the director. Some of the duties of an AD include keeping things running smoothly on the set, scheduling the shooting days, determining call times for cast and crew, dealing with extras, handling the various paperwork involved in the daily production, and so on. See also, *first assistant director; second assistant director.*

atmosphere   See *extra*.

available light   Any type of natural light, including sunlight, moonlight, and firelight. It refers to shooting in existing light sources without adding any artificial light. See also *artificial light*.

B & W   See *black-and-white*.

baby legs (baby tripod, babies)   A short tripod (Figure B.1a) used for low angle shots or any shots where the standard size tripod (Figure B.1b) is not appropriate.

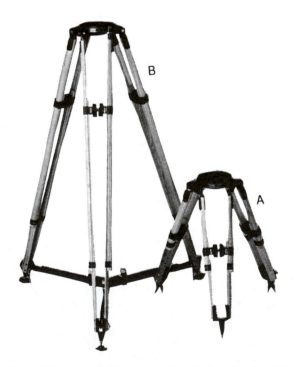

Figure B.1   O'Connor standard tripod and baby tripod. (a) baby tripod; (b) standard tripod. (Courtesy of O'Connor Camera Support Systems.)

background   See *extra*.

backlight   A light that is placed behind a subject or an object to highlight it and separate it from the background in the scene. A backlight may also be referred to as a *hairlight* when it is used to highlight an actor's hair. It sometimes creates a silhouette or halo effect. See also *hairlight*.

back lot   The area of the motion picture studio that is used when filming exterior scenes. It may include open-air areas or re-creations of various types of architecture necessary for the particular story being filmed. Sometimes the use of the back lot is necessary because it may be too costly to use actual locations or the location may no longer exist. Some back-lot sets are so realistic that the viewer may not be able to distinguish between shots filmed on a back lot and shots filmed on actual locations.

banana   A semicircular or curved movement an actor makes when moving from one position to another. Many times, it looks more realistic and natural for the actor to make this type of movement rather than to walk straight toward the camera.

barney   A flexible, padded, and insulated cover used to reduce noise coming from the camera or magazine. A heated version is used to keep the camera and magazine warm in extremely cold shooting situations.

barrel connector   A metal connector that allows two bnc cables to be connected in order to make a longer cable. When a video assist, monitor, and cables are rented from a camera rental house, a couple of barrel connectors should be obtained at the same time. Then if a situation arises where one length of video cable is not long enough, two or more cables can be joined to achieve the desired length.

base   One of the three main components that make up any piece of film stock. It is the smooth transparent surface to which the film emulsion is attached. In the earlier days of filmmaking, a nitrate base was used, which was highly flammable. Today, a safer acetate-type base is used for all film stocks (Figure A.2).

batch number   The number assigned by the manufacturer to a particular batch or emulsion of film stock when it is manufactured. It is usually advisable, when filming, to use film from the same batch number whenever possible so that you will have consistent color matching in the shots.

battery   Rechargeable power supply used to power the camera. Belt batteries and on-board batteries are usually used when doing hand-held shots. Block batteries are used when working on a dolly or tripod. Most camera batteries are either 12 volts or 24 volts, depending on the camera system being used. Some other types of batteries that may be

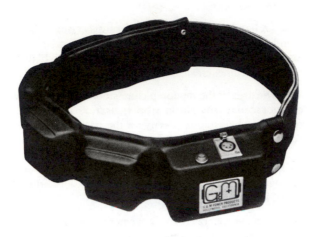

Figure B.2   G & M Universal Battery Belt. (Courtesy of G & M Power Products.)

used on the production include smaller-size batteries such as AA, AAA, C, and D that are used for any item that requires battery power, such as mini mag lights, flashlights, lighted magnifiers, and so on. These smaller batteries are usually purchased by the production company prior to filming.

battery belt   A belt containing the cells of the battery (Figure B.2), which may be worn by the operator or the assistant when doing hand-held shots. It may also be used when a block battery is impractical.

battery cable   Power cable that is used to connect the camera or any other accessory to the battery. It supplies the power from the battery to the camera or accessory being used.

battery charger   Electrical device used to keep the batteries fully charged when not being used. When charging, the battery is connected to the charger, and the charger is plugged into a standard 110 volt electrical outlet. The battery should never be connected to the camera while it is being charged.

below the line   The fixed costs incurred on a production that are not included in above-the-line costs. It also refers to the creative, technical personnel on a production. Below-the-line costs usually include wages paid to the crew, film-stock purchases, laboratory fees for processing film, equipment rental, studio rental, travel expenses, and location expenses. Below-the-line personnel usually include all members of the technical crew, such as the camera crew, grip and lighting crews, property personnel, makeup and wardrobe people, and so on.

belt battery   A battery held in a battery belt. See also *battery belt*.

black-and-white (B&W)   Any film that is shot without using color film. Sometimes a film is shot in color film and, during the developing and printing process, the color is taken away to give a black-and-white image.

black bag   A small plastic or paper bag that contains the raw film stock when it is inside the film can. After the film has been exposed, it is placed back in the black bag and then in the film can, which is sealed for delivery to the lab. Some camera assistants also refer to the *changing bag* as the *black bag*, but it is not the same as the one used for wrapping the film.

black dot texture screen   A diffusion filter, which looks like a clear piece of glass, that contains small black dots in a random pattern. These black dots cause the light striking them to become spread out over a large area, which causes the image to appear diffused and out of focus. They come in a set ranging from number 1, which is the lightest, to number 5, which is the heaviest. It requires an exposure compensation of one stop.

blimp   A soundproof housing in which the camera is placed to prevent any camera noise from getting on the sound track during sync sound filming. Many of the earlier cameras had to be placed in blimps because they were so loud, but today's newer cameras are self-blimped.

block battery   A large camera battery that is enclosed in some type of case containing the cells of the battery as well as a built-in charger. Block batteries may come in single blocks, containing only one battery, or dual blocks, containing two batteries (Figures B.3, B.4).

blower bulb syringe   A rubber device that is used to remove any dust particles from the lens or filter. Squeezing the bulb repeatedly expels air, which blows away any dust from the lens or filter. Some assistants prefer to use the blower bulb instead of the compressed air can. Both will do the same job.

bnc cables   See *video cables*.

Bolex   Trade name for a brand of 16mm motion picture camera.

boom shot   A type of continuous shot usually done from some type of camera crane or boom and including many different camera angles. The shot may start with a low-angle shot and, by extending the boom

Figure B.3   G & M Dual Battery Pack. (Courtesy of G & M Power Products.)

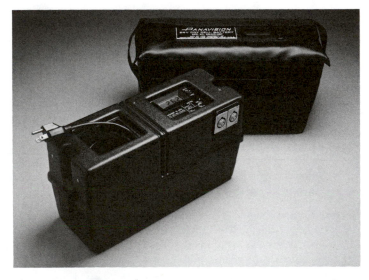

Figure B.4   Panavision purse-style block battery. (Courtesy of Panavision, Inc.)

or crane, continue up to a high-angle shot. The shot may also be the reverse, starting high and ending low.

box rental   Also called **kit rental**. The fee paid to a member of the technical crew for the use of their personal tools and equipment on a production. This fee is usually paid on a weekly or daily basis.

breathing (lens)   A property of a zoom lens that causes it to appear to change focal length while the focus is being adjusted. It is a problem that is inherent to some zoom lenses and cannot be fixed or changed. Not all zoom lenses have this problem, and it is best to use a lens that does not breathe, whenever possible.

bubble level   A small circular level used to precisely set the balance and level of the camera when it is placed on an uneven surface.

cable   Any set of wires or connectors that may be joined to a battery to supply power to a camera or zoom or to power a heater or any other similar application.

call   The time that the cast and crew must report to work for the day's shooting. The call time is usually determined by the first assistant director and is based on the wrap time of the previous day's shooting. Each member of the cast and crew is given a call sheet that lists the call time as well as the scenes and equipment needed for each day's filming. See also *call sheet*.

call sheet   A production form given to each member of the cast and crew at the end of each shooting day. It contains all pertinent information regarding the next day's shooting. Some of the information includes the call time for each cast and crew member, scenes to be shot and the actors needed for each scene, any special equipment needs, location of shooting, and so on (Figures C.1, C.2).

camera   The basic piece of equipment used to photograph the images. All cameras consist of a lens, which projects the image onto the film stock; a shutter, which regulates the light striking the film; a viewfinder, which enables the camera operator to view the image during filming; some type of mechanism to transport the film through the camera; a motor to power the camera; and a light-proof container, called a magazine, that holds the film before and after exposure (Figures A.3– A.7, P.1–P.3).

camera angle   The position, or point of view, of the camera during filming. The camera angle determines what will be included in the shot, and it is usually determined by the director of photography based on what feeling the director is trying to convey in the scene. Some typical camera angles include eye level, high angle, low angle, and Dutch angle. The eye-level shot is the most realistic and lifelike because it provides a normal view of the scene. The high-angle shot is filmed

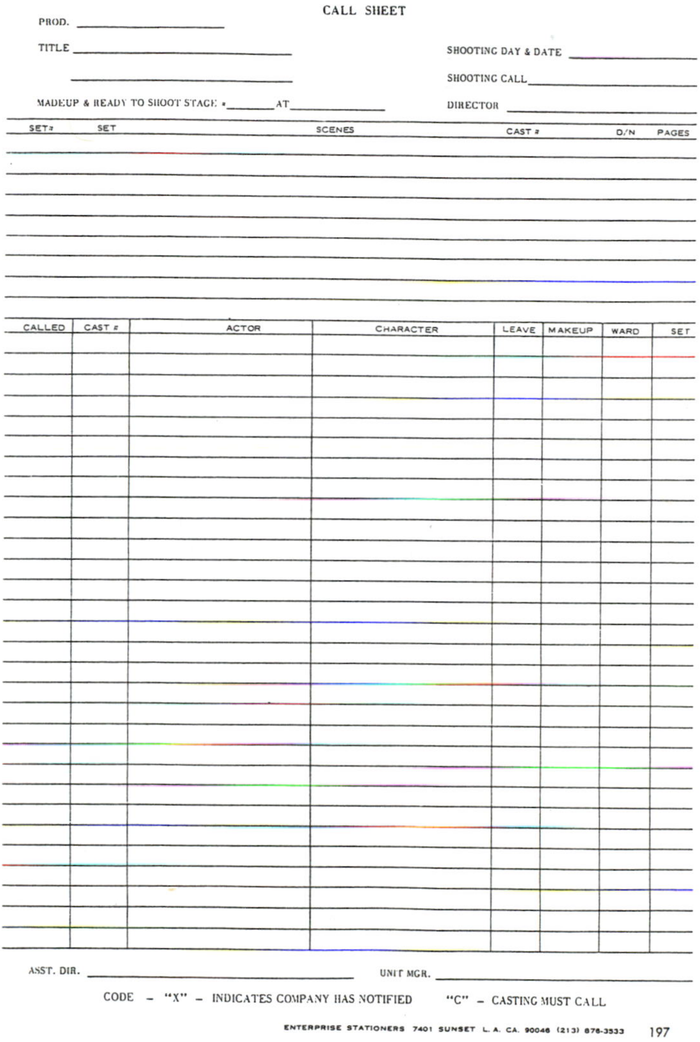

CALL SHEET

PROD. _____

TITLE _____

_____

MADEUP & READY TO SHOOT STAGE #_____ AT_____

SHOOTING DAY & DATE _____

SHOOTING CALL_____

DIRECTOR _____

SET#	SET	SCENES	CAST #	D/N	PAGES

CALLED	CAST #	ACTOR	CHARACTER	LEAVE	MAKEUP	WARD	SET

ASST. DIR. _____   UNIT MGR. _____

CODE — "X" — INDICATES COMPANY HAS NOTIFIED   "C" — CASTING MUST CALL

ENTERPRISE STATIONERS 7401 SUNSET L.A. CA. 90046 (213) 876-3533   197

Figure C.1 Front page of standard call sheet.

from above the action of the scene, and a low-angle shot is filmed from below the action of the scene. A *Dutch* angle requires that the camera be tilted in an unrealistic manner so that the action is happening diagonally within the frame. The proper camera angle can help to set the mood of the scene or emphasize a particular element in the scene. It also may determine how the audience views the scene. When cutting

DATE _____

TITLE _____

WORK ORDER

PROD. # _____

CREW CALL _____
(UNLESS OTHERWISE NOTED)

NO.	PRODUCTION	TIME	NO.	ELECTRIC	TIME	NO.	WARDROBE	TIME
	SCRIPT SUPERVISOR			GAFFER			WARD. DESIGNER	
	TECH. ADVISOR			BEST BOY			MEN'S COSTUME	
				ELECTRICIANS			WOMEN'S COSTUME	
	CAMERA			LOCAL #40 MAN				
	CAMERAMAN			SIGNAL LITES				
	OPERATOR			GEN. OPER.			FACILITIES DIVISION / SECURITY	
	1ST ASST.			WIND MACH. OPER.				
	2ND ASST.	/		HOOKUP MU & DR'S BY				
	STILLMAN			GENERATOR				
	EXTRA OPERATOR						HOSPITAL	
	EXTRA 1ST ASST.							
	EXTRA 2ND ASST.							
	SOUND						CONSTRUCTION	
	MIXER						1ST GRIP	
	BOOMMAN			MEALS			2ND GRIP	
	RECORDER			HOT MEALS			DOLLY GRIP	
	CABLEMAN			COFFEE & DONUTS			BOOM CREW	
	P.B. & OPER.			TABLES & CHAIRS			GRIPS	
	VOICE GUNS			MOBILE KITCHEN			SPEC. EFX. MAN	
	PHONE HOOKUP						POWDER MAN	
	P.A. SYSTEM						GREENSMAN	
				LOCATION			SERVICEMAN	
							PAINTER	
	PROPERTY							
	PROPMASTER							
	ASST. PROPMAN			PROCESS EDIT.			CRAB DOLLY	
	EXTRA PROPMAN			A.E. PORT. & OPER.			HYDR. TRIPOD	
	DECORATORS			PROJECTIONIST			RO CRANE	
	WRGLRS.			PROC. B.G'S			BOOM	
	ANIMAL HDLRS.			STEREO PLATES			WESTERN DOLLY	
	A.H.A. REPR.			FILM ED-NEC. FILM			SCHOOLROOM	
	MU TABLES						BENCHES	
	SCHOOLRM SETUP			MUSIC			DR'S	
	HEATER'S IN DR'S						CK ROOM	
							RG'S	
	WARD. RACKS			MAKEUP			DARKROOM ?	
	CK. OR SETUP			MU MAN			KD'S	
				MU MAN				
				HAIRDRESSER			TR DR UNIT	
	LIVESTOCK-WAGONS			BODY MU			TR DR UNIT	
				ENGINEERING				
				CONDITION STAGE				
	SPECIAL INSTR. OR REQUIREMENTS							

TRANSPORTATION/PICTURE CARS

ASSISTANT DIRECTOR   UNIT MANAGER

Figure C.2   Back page of standard call sheet.

within a scene, it is important to keep the camera angles correct so that the edited picture looks correct when viewed.

camera assistant (AC)   A member of the camera crew who works closely with the director of photography and camera operator during the shooting day. Some of the job responsibilities include maintaining and setting up the camera, changing lenses, loading film, measuring focus distances, focusing and zooming during the shot, clapping the slate, keeping camera reports and other paperwork, and so on. The camera department usually consists of the first camera assistant (1st AC) and the second camera assistant (2nd AC). See also *first camera assistant; second camera assistant.*

camera car   A specially constructed vehicle containing a variety of mounts on which the camera can be placed for filming many types of driving shots involving a moving vehicle (Figure C.3). The camera may be mounted on the front, rear, side, or top of the vehicle or may even be attached to a crane that is part of the camera car. The vehicle being photographed is sometimes being towed by the camera car to make filming appear more realistic without jeopardizing the actors. The camera car is designed to carry key production personnel during the filming of these moving shots.

camera crew   The department on a film production usually consisting of the director of photography, camera operator, first camera assistant, and second camera assistant. The camera crew is responsible for the photography of the film and maintenance of all camera equipment. On many larger productions, the camera crew may also have a film loader as one of the positions.

camera, hand-held   A camera that has been set up so that it may be held on the camera operator's shoulders during filming (Figures C.4, C.5). It may be used to film moving shots or point-of-view shots of an actor walking or moving through the scene. When filming hand-held shots, it is customary to have a wide-angle lens on the camera, which helps to minimize the shakiness associated with these shots. When ordering the camera equipment, smaller magazines should be ordered, along with other special accessories such as hand grips and shoulder pads, if any hand-held shots are to be done. The smaller magazines reduce

Figure C.3   Shotmaker Classic camera car. (Courtesy of Camera Platforms International, Inc.)

Figure C.4   Arriflex 535 camera in hand-held configuration. (Photo courtesy of the Arriflex Corporation.)

Figure C.5   Panavision Platinum camera in hand-held configuration. (Courtesy of Panavision, Inc.)

the weight of the camera, making it easier for the operator to carry the camera during filming.

camera jam   A malfunction that occurs when the film backs up in the camera and becomes piled up in the camera movement. The film usually becomes caught between the sprocket wheels and the guide rollers. This may be caused by torn perforations or improper threading in the camera or magazine. Torn perforations may cause the film to not engage on the sprockets properly. Improper threading may create a film loop that is too large or too small, causing the camera motor to work harder to move the film through the camera. This extra pressure on the motor may result in the film jamming in the camera. See also *magazine jam.*

camera left   The area to the left side of the camera as seen from the camera operator's point of view. As the actor faces the camera, camera left is to the actor's right.

cameraman   See *director of photography.*

camera mount   Any type of device on which the camera is mounted for support. The camera may be attached to a head and placed on a dolly, tripod, high hat, camera car, and so on.

camera oil   A special type of oil used for lubricating the movement in the camera. It is usually supplied by the camera rental house or camera manufacturer. Only the recommended camera oil should be used for a particular camera; Panavision oil should never be used on an Arriflex camera or Arriflex oil on a Panavision camera.

camera operator (operator)   The member of the camera crew who looks through and operates the camera during filming. He maintains the composition of the shot, as instructed by the director and director of photography, by making smooth pan and tilt moves. The camera operator is usually the only person who sees the actual shot during filming and can approve the take or request another shot if it seems necessary.

camera prep   See *prep.*

camera rental house   A company that specializes in the rental and maintenance of motion picture camera equipment.

camera report   A form that is filled in with the pertinent information for each roll of film shot. It includes all production information such as company, title, director's name, and director of photography's name. It should also have spaces for the magazine number, roll number, amount of film in the magazine, emulsion number, date of shot, and scene and take numbers. It also lists the length of each shot expressed in feet, the amount of film used, which takes are good or no good, and any instructions to the lab regarding developing instructions. Most camera reports are usually one of three styles as shown in Figures C.6–C.8.

camera right   The area to the right side of camera as seen from the camera operator's point of view. As the actor faces the camera, *camera right* is to the actor's left.

camera speed   The rate at which the film is transported through the camera during filming. It is expressed in frames per second, abbreviated fps. Normal sync camera speed in the United States is 24 fps.

camera tape   Cloth tape, usually one inch in width, that is used for making labels on cases, film cans, and magazines and any other labels that may be required. It is also used for wrapping cans of exposed film and unexposed film and short ends. It may be used by the first camera assistant for focus marks on the ground. The most commonly used colors of camera tape are white and black, but it is also available in red, yellow, orange, blue, and gray.

camera truck   A large enclosed truck used to transport and store all camera equipment when filming on location. It is usually set up with a workbench, shelves for storage of equipment, and a darkroom for loading and unloading film (Figure C.9).

camera wedge   A small wooden wedge that may be used to help level the camera when it is placed on uneven surfaces.

Cartoni   Trade name for a brand of fluid camera heads and tripods. Some of the models of fluid heads include the *C10*, *C20*, *C40*, *Beta*, and *Cartoni Dutch Head*.

CC   See *color compensating filter*.

Century Precision Optics   Manufacturer of specialty lenses, lens accessories, and lens attachments.

chamois   Special type of leather cloth used for cleaning camera and magazines.

champagne roll   A term usually used to refer to the 100th roll of film used during filming. It received its name because the production company usually provides bottles of champagne to celebrate when this roll is placed on the camera.

changing bag   A lightproof cloth bag used to load and unload film when a darkroom is not available. It is actually two bags sewn together, one inside the other. At the top of each bag is a zipper that gives access to the inside of the bag. It also contains two sleeves containing elastic

deluxe laboratories, inc.

1377 NORTH SERRANO AVE., HOLLYWOOD, CA 90027 • PHONE 462-6171

camera report
sound report

DATE _____ CUSTOMER ORDER NUMBER _____

COMPANY _____

DIRECTOR _____ CAMERAMAN / RECORDIST _____

PRODUCTION NUMBER OR TITLE _____

MAGAZINE NUMBER _____ ROLL NUMBER _____

TYPE OF FILM AND TYPE OF DAILIES
PLEASE CIRCLE

35 MM COLOR	35 MM B/W	16 MM COLOR	16 MM B/W
ONE LIGHT	ONE LIGHT	ONE LIGHT	ONE LIGHT
TIMED DAILIES	TIMED DAILIES	TIMED DAILIES	TIMED DAILIES

FORCE DEVELOP: ONE STOP   TWO STOPS

TYPE OF FILM / EMULSION _____

PRINT CIRCLED TAKES ONLY:

SCENE NUMBER	TAKES				REMARKS	
	1 '	2 '	3 '	4 '	DAY OR NIGHT	INTERIOR OR EXTERIOR

TOTAL FOOTAGE _____

All contracts with this company are accepted with the understanding that all film delivered to it is covered by the owner against loss. This company takes every necessary precaution for the safekeeping of the film, but assumes no responsibility for its loss.

DEL 82 Rev. 7-76

Figure C.6 Deluxe Labs camera report. (Courtesy of Deluxe Laboratories, Inc.)

Company							**CAMERA**					
Pic. Title				Prod. No.			**REPORT**					
Director							Customer Order No.					
Cameraman				Cam. No.			Sheet No.			of		
Mag No.				Roll No.				**FOTO-KEM**				
Footage				Date Exposed				Industries, Inc.				
Film type				Emulsion No.				2800 West Olive Avenue				
Develop	□ Normal		□ Other					Burbank, California 91505 (818) 846-3101				

SCENE NO.	TAKE	DIAL	FEET	SD.	REMARKS	SCENE NO.	TAKE	DIAL	FEET	SD.	REMARKS
										G	
										NG	
										W	
										T	

Figure C.7 Foto-Kem camera report. (Courtesy of Foto-Kem Industries, Inc.)

cuffs, on the opposite side of the bag from the zippers. The magazine is placed inside the inner bag and both zippers are then closed. With the zippers closed and the assistant's arms placed inside the sleeves, it forms a lightproof compartment for loading and unloading the film stock.

changing tent Very similar in design to a changing bag except that it forms a dome-shaped tent over the working surface. It is constructed of two layers, similar to the construction of the changing bag, and contains a double zippered door, with one sleeve on each side of the door (Figure C.10).

Chapman Trade name for a brand of camera dolly and camera crane (Figures C.14, C.15, and D.9).

cheat To change the position of the camera, actors, or props with relation to the background. The director may request a particular shot and, by cheating the positions with relation to the master shot, can get the

CAMERA REPORT

Technicolor®

4050 LANKERSHIM BLVD.
N. HOLLYWOOD, CALIF. 91608

(818) 769-8500

Telex 674108

PROD. COMPANY/# _____

FILM TITLE _____ DATE _____

CAMERAMAN _____ DIRECTOR _____

CAMERA I.D. _____ MAG. NO. _____ ROLL # _____

☐ 35 mm. ☐ Color ☐ One Light
☐ 16 mm. ☐ B & W ☐ Timed

Type of Film/Emulsion _____

Processing — Normal ☐ Forced 1 Stop ☐ Forced 2 Stop ☐

SCENE NO.	TAKE	DIAL	PRINT	DAY / NIGHT	INT. / EXT.	REMARKS
						FOOTAGE
						GOOD
						N.G.
						WASTE
						TOTAL

Form 758

Technicolor is a Registered Trademark

Figure C.8 Technicolor camera report. (Courtesy of Technicolor Labs.)

Figure C.9 Detailed view of interior of camera truck. (Reprinted from *The ARRI 35 Book*, with permission of the Arriflex Corporation.)

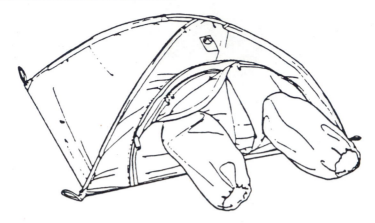

Figure C.10   Harrison changing tent. (Reprinted from *The ARRI 35 Book*, with permission of the Arriflex Corporation.)

required shot. This may be done in order to have a more appealing background or to remove unsightly objects that are in the frame.

checking the gate   The procedure done by the first camera assistant, after each printed take, to determine if there is any hair, or film emulsion, stuck in the gate. The hair is not a human hair, but rather a very fine piece of film emulsion that may have been scraped off during filming. If a hair is found, it is usually customary to request an additional take. See also *hair*.

choker   A tight close-up shot that frames the actor's face very closely, usually having the bottom frame line at the actor's neckline.

chopping   A slang term used to refer to the location of the frame lines on the actor or on object being photographed. An actor may ask the cameraman, "Where are you chopping me?"

Chrosziel   Trade name of a brand of motion picture camera equipment, including matte boxes and follow focus mechanisms.

Cinema Products   The manufacturer of many specialized pieces of motion picture equipment. These include the *Steadicam, Worral,* and *Mini Worral Geared Heads*.

Cinemascope   Trade name given to the wide-screen filming process that has an aspect ratio of 2.35 to 1 (2.35:1).

cinematographer   See *director of photography*.

cinematography   The art and craft of recording images on motion picture film.

Cinematography Electronics   Manufacturer of a brand of motion picture camera-speed-control devices. These include the *16SR Speed Control, HMI & TV Crystal Control, Precision Speed Control, ARRI 2C Crystal Base,* and *ARRI 35-3 Crystal Base.*

Cine 60   Trade name for a brand of camera batteries.

clapper   See *clap sticks.*

clapper boards   See *clap sticks.*

clapper/loader   A member of the camera crew who is responsible for clapping the slate for the shot and also for loading and unloading the film in the magazines. This term is used primarily in Britain and Europe. In the United States, it is the second camera assistant.

clapper sticks   See *clap sticks.*

clap sticks   The wooden sticks attached to the slate that are clapped together at the beginning of a sync sound take. See also *slate.*

clean single   A single shot of an actor framed so that there is no other actor or part of an actor in the shot.

closed set   A film set on a stage or on location that is closed to any visitors or nonessential crew members. Many times when an intimate scene is being photographed, only the key, essential crew members are permitted to remain on the set.

close-up (CU)   A shot that shows a great amount of detail in an object or an actor; usually done with a very long focal length lens. A close-up of an actor would usually include the head and shoulders.

closing down the lens   Also called *stopping down the lens.* Turning the diaphragm-adjustment ring of the lens to a higher f-stop number, which results in a smaller diaphragm opening and allows less light to strike the film.

coaxial cable   See *video cables.*

coaxial magazine   A film magazine that contains two distinct compartments, one for the feed side and another for the take-up side (Figure C.11). *Coaxial* refers to the fact that these two distinct compartments share the same axis of rotation. When loading a coaxial magazine, the feed side must be loaded in the dark, and the take-up side may be loaded in the light. When unloading a coaxial magazine, the take-up side must be done in the dark, and the feed side may be done in the light as long as there is no short end remaining in the feed side.

collapsible core   A permanent core in the take-up side of the film magazine onto which the film is wound as it is being exposed. The end of

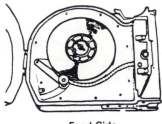

Feed Side

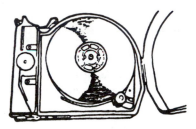

Take-up Side

Figure C.11 Arriflex 16SR coaxial magazine showing threading pattern. (Reprinted from *The 16SR Book*, with permission of the Arriflex Corporation.)

the film slips into a slot cut in the core and is held in place by a small locking lever that pinches the end of the film against the inside of the core (Figure C.12). When the locking lever is engaged, the core expands slightly. When unloading the exposed film, the locking lever is released, and the core collapses slightly in size, which allows easy removal of the roll of film.

color chart   A card that shows strips of colors corresponding to the colors of the spectrum and that is used by the lab to assist in developing and processing the film.

color compensating filter (CC)   A filter used to make very small adjustments in the color temperature of the light as it strikes the film. It comes in the primary and complementary colors and in varying densities. A CC requires an exposure compensation depending on the color and density of the filter.

color grad filter   A filter that is half color and half clear, used when a specific color effect is desired.

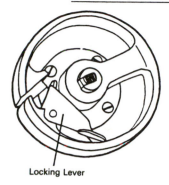

Locking Lever

Figure C.12   Collapsible core.

color sensitivity   The degree of accuracy with which a particular film stock reproduces various colors.

color temperature   A measurement or scale in degrees Kelvin (K) that measures the specific color of a light.

combination filter   A filter that is made from the combination of two different filter types, for example, an 85 combined with a neutral density (85N3, 85N6, 85N9) or an 85 combined with a polarizer (85POLA). The most commonly used combination filters are the 85 combined with a neutral density. The exposure compensation for a combination filter is the total of the exposure compensations for each individual filter; for example, when using an 85N3, the exposure compensation would be one and two-thirds stops—one stop for the ND3 and two-thirds stop for the 85.

commissary   The restaurant or cafeteria located on the lot of a major studio.

"Common marker"   Also called *"Common slate."* What the second camera assistant calls out when slating a shot for two or more cameras by using only one slate. When using only one slate, all cameras point toward the slate at the beginning of the shot. Once the sound is rolling, the cameras are started and are slated at the same time.

"Common slate"   See *"Common marker."*

complementary colors   For the purposes of cinematography, yellow, cyan, and magenta. They are produced when two of the primary colors, blue, red, and green, are combined: red + blue = magenta, red + green = yellow, and green + blue = cyan. Yellow, cyan, and magenta are the complements of the primary colors, blue, red, and green, respectively. See also *primary colors.*

compressed air   Canned air used to blow out the magazine and camera body, and also to clean dust off lenses and filters. Some types of compressed air contain fluorocarbons, which harm the atmosphere; if possible, they should not be used. A newer type of compressed air claims to have no harmful fluorocarbons and so is considered safe for the environment.

contrast   The difference between the light areas and dark areas within a scene.

conversion filter   A filter used to convert one color temperature to another. The two most common conversion filters are the 85 and the 80A. The 85 converts tungsten-balanced film for use in daylight, and the 80A filter converts daylight-balanced film for use in tungsten light. See also *80A filter; 85 filter.*

coral filter   A filter used to warm up the overall scene and to enhance skin tones. It is also used to make slight adjustments in Kelvin temperature for different times of day. It requires an exposure compensation depending on the density of the filter.

core   Plastic disks around which raw stock film is wound (Figure C.13). They can be either 2 or 3 inches in diameter.

cotton swab   A long wooden stick with a small piece of cotton wrapped around one end; can be used to remove excess oil when oiling the camera.

coverage (coverage shot)   Filming a scene from many different camera angles. This allows the scene to be viewed from different points of view. When the various shots are edited together, the different coverage helps to set the mood or tone for the scene.

cover set   A set that is used as a standby in case the original set scheduled for shooting cannot be used. A cover set may be used if there is a change in weather or if one of the actors becomes ill.

16MM   35MM

Figure C.13   Plastic film cores.

cowboy shot   A shot that frames the actor from just above the knees to the top of the head. The name comes from the early-western practice of including the cowboy's gun holster, which hung to just above the knees, in the shot.

crab dolly   A four-wheeled device on which the camera may be mounted, allowing the filming of complicated moving shots. The dolly may be moved in any direction.

craft service   The member of the film crew who is responsible for setting up and maintaining the wide variety of snacks and drinks available to the crew during shooting. This person also is responsible for keeping the area around the set clean and free from litter.

crane   A large-wheeled vehicle on which the camera is mounted, allowing the filming of continuous shots from very high angles (Figures C.14, C.15). It contains a long boom arm that allows the camera to be placed

Figure C.14   Chapman Super Nova mobile crane. (Courtesy of Chapman Leonard Studio Equipment.)

Figure C.15 Chapman Zeus stage crane. (Courtesy of Chapman Leonard Studio Equipment.)

in many different positions during filming. It can usually carry the camera and two people, including the camera operator and first camera assistant. The crane is usually operated by members of the grip crew.

crew call The time at which the crew must report to work for the day's shooting.

cross hairs Perpendicular lines, that is, a cross, that are etched into the ground glass of the camera's viewing system. The cross is in the exact center of the film frame to assist the camera operator in framing the shot (Figure C.16).

crystal motor The most common type of motor for motion picture cameras. A built-in crystal allows the motor to run at precise speeds, especially when filming with sound, without the use of a cable running from the camera to the sound recorder. Many crystal motors can be set to different speeds for various shooting situations such as high speed or slow motion.

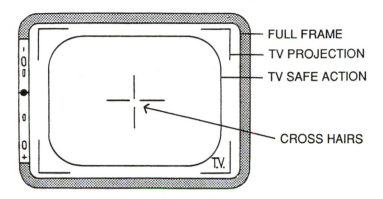

Figure C.16   Ground glass showing frame lines and cross hairs. (Reprinted from *The 16SR Book*, with permission of the Arriflex Corporation.)

CU   Abbreviation for *close-up*.

cube tap   Electrical attachment that is used to connect three different items to one electrical outlet.

"cut"   What the director calls out when he wants the actors to stop their performance or when he wants the action of the scene to end. It is also the signal for the sound recordist and camera operator to turn off the sound recorder and camera.

cutaway   A shot used by the editor to get away from the main action in the scene. It may be an insert of an item being talked about or a reaction of someone in the scene.

dailies Also called **rushes**. The developed and printed scenes from the previous day's filming that are viewed by the key production personnel each day. They are usually viewed by the director, director of photography, camera operator, first camera assistant, editor, and so on.

daily film inventory A form for recording information relating to how much film is shot each day. It lists all film stocks and roll numbers used for the day, with a breakdown of good and no-good takes, waste footage, and any short ends made. It also shows how much film is on hand at the end of each day's shooting. Each camera assistant usually has his or her own style of inventory form that they prefer to use (Figures D.1–D.3).

darkroom A small, lightproof room (usually 4 ft by 4 ft in size), on a stage or in a camera truck, that is used for the loading and unloading of film (Figure D.4). The unexposed raw stock film is usually stored in the darkroom during production.

day for night The technique of filming a night sequence during the day. The exterior night effect is achieved by placing certain filters on the camera. This technique is rarely used because it usually looks too unrealistic. If possible, it is much better to wait until dark to film any night shots.

daylight A light source with a color temperature of approximately 5600 K.

daylight spool A special film reel, usually made of metal or plastic with opaque edges, that allows film to be loaded into the camera in daylight (Figure D.5). Only the outer layers of the film are exposed to the light. The daylight spool is most commonly used in 16mm cinematography but may sometimes be used for 35mm filming.

day player An actor or technician who is hired only for one day's work. The actor may be in only one scene or have only a few lines. The

PRODUCTION _____ DATE _____

FILM STOCK _____

ROLL #	GOOD	N.G.	WASTE	TOTAL (1)	S.E.	TOTAL (2)

TOTALS	GOOD	N.G.	WASTE	TOTAL (1)	FILM ON HAND	
TODAY					PREVIOUS	
PREVIOUS					TODAY (+)	
TOTAL					TODAY (-)	
					TOTAL	

FILM STOCK _____

ROLL #	GOOD	N.G.	WASTE	TOTAL (1)	S.E.	TOTAL (2)

TOTALS	GOOD	N.G.	WASTE	TOTAL (1)	FILM ON HAND	
TODAY					PREVIOUS	
PREVIOUS					TODAY (+)	
TOTAL					TODAY (-)	
					TOTAL	

TOTAL FILM USE	GOOD	N.G.	WASTE	TOTAL	TOTAL FILM ON HAND	
TODAY					PREVIOUS	
PREVIOUS					TODAY (+)	
TOTAL					TODAY (-)	
					TOTAL	

Figure D.1   Daily film inventory form #1.

technician may be hired to replace another technician for the day or may be needed because additional equipment is being used for the day's filming.

deal memo   A production form completed by actors and technicians that outlines the terms of the work assignment and the amount of compen-

PRODUCTION _____

DATE _____

FILM TYPE	LOAD TYPE	ROLL	GOOD	N.G.	WASTE	TOTAL

			GOOD	N.G.	WASTE	TOTAL
		PREVIOUS				
		TODAY (+)				
		TO DATE				
	TOTAL EXP.				UNEXP. ON HAND	

	FILM			FILM					TOTAL
	1000' LOADS	400' LOADS		1000' LOADS	400' LOADS		ON HAND	ON HAND	ON HAND
PREVIOUS									
TODAY (−)									
TODAY (+)									
TO DATE ON HAND									

Figure D.2   Daily film inventory form #2.

sation for that assignment (Figure D.6). It lists the number of hours to be worked, the basic pay rate and overtime rate, and any rental fees that are paid to the technician. Upon completion of the deal memo, it should be signed by the employee and a representative of the production company.

depth of field   The range of distance in front of and behind the principle point of focus within which all objects will be in acceptable sharp focus (Figure D.7). There is usually more depth of field behind the point of focus than there is in front of it. The depth of field is determined by

DAILY FILM INVENTORY

Date _____   Prod. No. _____

Production _____

NEG.	ROLL	AMOUNT	GOOD	N/G	WASTE	TOTAL	S.E.
TOTALS							

	( )	( )	( )	TOTAL
BALANCE				
(+) REC'D. TODAY				
BALANCE				
(−) USED TODAY				
BALANCE				

Figure D.3 Daily film inventory form #3.

three factors, the focal length of the lens, the f-stop used, and the distance that the object is from the camera.

DGA See *Directors Guild of America*.

diaphragm The adjustable metal blades that control the amount of light entering the lens. Turning the barrel of the lens to set the f-stop adjusts the diaphragm within the lens. See also *iris*.

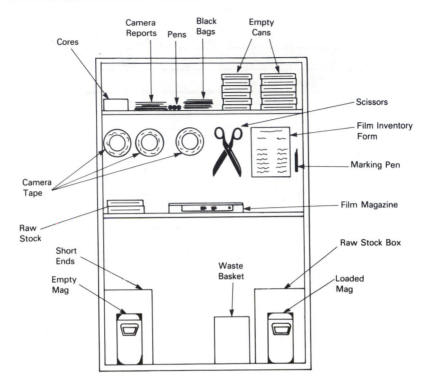

Figure D.4   Typical setup for darkroom.

Figure D.5   Daylight spool.

DEAL MEMO

PRODUCTION COMPANY:_____

ADDRESS: _____

CITY: _____ STATE: ___ ZIP:_____

TELEPHONE: _____

PRODUCTION TITLE: _____

EMPLOYEE NAME: _____

ADDRESS: _____

CITY: _____ STATE: ___ ZIP:_____

TELEPHONE: _____ S.S. NUMBER: _____

START DATE: _____ JOB TITLE:_____

       RATE:_____ PER:_____ DAY_____ WEEK

       GUARANTEED HOURS:_____ PER:_____ DAY_____ WEEK

       BOX OR KIT RENTAL:_____ PER:_____ DAY_____ WEEK

       PER DIEM:_____ PER:_____ DAY_____ WEEK

       TRAVEL: _____

       EXPENSES: _____

       OTHER:_____

                   _____

AGREED AND ACCEPTED:

_____

EMPLOYEE SIGNATURE

_____

PRODUCTION MANAGER

Figure D.6   Typical production deal memo.

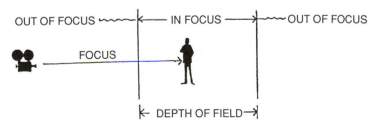

Figure D.7   Diagram illustrating the principle of depth of field.

diffusion filter   A filter that is used to slightly decrease the sharpness of the image. It is very good for smoothing out facial blemishes or wrinkles and for dreamlike effects. When used, this filter may give the appearance that the image is out of focus. Diffusion filters are available in various densities from very light to very heavy, and most require no exposure compensation.

DIN   The abbreviation for *Deutsche Industrie Norm*.

DIN number   A number assigned to each film stock to indicate the film stock's sensitivity to light, or film speed, in the German system. It may be used in place of *ASA number* or *EI*. See also *ASA number; exposure index*.

diopter   A filter that allows focusing on something much closer than the lens would normally handle. They are available in various strengths—the higher the number of the diopter, the closer you can focus. A diopter requires no exposure compensation.

director   The person responsible for all creative aspects of a production. The director determines how the script will be translated from the written word to the screen. He works closely with the actors, instructing them how to deliver their lines and how to move and react for each individual scene. The director discusses the shots with the director of photography to determine the position of the camera and the lens that might be used.

director of photography (DP)   Also called **cameraman; cinematographer**. The person in charge of lighting the set and photographing a film. He works closely with the director to transform the written words of the script to the screen, based on the director's vision. The DP oversees all aspects of the camera department and the camera crew. The DP supervises all technical crews on a production during filming.

Directors Guild of America (DGA)   The union to which directors, assistant directors, and production managers belong.

director's viewfinder   A viewing device that allows the director to frame up the precise shot without the use of the camera. The standard director's viewfinder has two dials, one that corresponds to the various aspect ratios and the other that corresponds to the various focal lengths of the lenses. By setting the proper aspect ratio and then dialing in the correct lens size, the director can view exactly how the shot will look through the lens. There are also viewfinders available that are made so that the actual lens may be attached, and the shot lined up.

dirty single   A shot of a single actor that is framed in such a way to include a small part of another actor in the scene. You may only see the hair or part of the shoulder of the other actor.

displacement magazine   A magazine that contains the feed and take-up sides on the same side of the magazine. When the magazine is placed on the camera, the feed side is toward the front, and the take-up side is toward the rear. As the film runs through the camera, it is displaced from the feed side to the take-up side. A displacement magazine may be of the single-chamber type (Figure D.8), which contains both the feed and take-up in the same compartment and requires that the entire loading and unloading process be done in complete darkness; or the double chamber type, which has separate compartments for the feed and take-up sides. The double-chamber displacement magazine may be loaded and unloaded in a similar fashion as the coaxial magazine.

ditty bag   A canvas bag containing many different-sized compartments that is used by the camera assistant to hold his tools and supplies needed for filming. Some of the items kept in the ditty bag include basic tools, the slate, tape measure, pens, permanent felt markers, camera tape, and so on.

dolly   A four-wheeled platform on which to mount the camera for moving shots (Figures D.9–D.11). It may also have a boom arm that allows the camera to be raised or lowered for a shot. The dolly allows the camera to be moved in any direction during the shot. It usually contains seats for the camera operator and camera assistant to sit on during filming. It is operated by a crew member known as the dolly grip. See also *crab dolly; crane.*

dolly grip   The member of the grip crew who is responsible for maintaining the camera dolly and moving it during the shots. He works closely with the camera operator during rehearsals to ensure smooth dolly moves and boom-arm moves for the shot. See also *grip.*

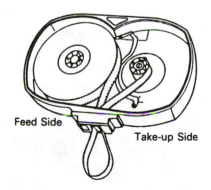

Feed Side

Take-up Side

Figure D.8   Panavision 35mm displacement magazine showing threading pattern. (Courtesy of Panavision, Inc.)

Figure D.9   Chapman HUSTLER dolly. (Courtesy of Chapman
Leonard Studio Equipment.)

Figure D.10   Fisher Model TEN dolly. (Courtesy of J. L. Fisher Inc.)

Figure D.11   Super Panther dolly. (Courtesy of Panther
Corporation of America.)

dolly in   See *dolly shot*.

dolly out   See *dolly shot*.

dolly shot   Any type of moving shot that is done from the dolly. The dolly
may be placed on some type of tracks to allow for smooth shots. A
dolly-in means that the camera gets closer to the action. A *dolly-out*
means that the camera gets farther away from the action.

donut   Also called **rubber donut**. A circular piece of rubber approximately
1/2-inch thick with a circular hole cut out of the center. A donut comes
in various diameters. It is placed on the front of the lens to seal the
opening between the lens and the matte box, thus preventing any

light from entering the matte box from behind the lens and reflecting off the filters and into the lens.

double   Also called **photo double**. A performer who takes the place of the principal actor in the shot. The double usually resembles the actor in height and physical appearance and is often the same person as the stand-in. The double may be used in shots when you do not need to see the actor up close—long shots, crowd scenes, or some types of driving scenes. The double may be a stunt person because of a difficult or dangerous stunt involved.

DP   See *director of photography*.

drive-on   A pass issued by the security department at a studio that allows a person to drive his/her vehicle onto the studio lot. A drive-on pass may be issued to an actor or technician or any other employee who is working at the studio or to someone visiting at the studio.

drive-to money   See *mileage*.

dulling spray   A spray that is used to dull down any shiny or bright objects in the shot. It is not permanent and can be easily wiped off when done.

dummy load   A short roll of raw stock film that is too small to be used for photographing any shots. It may be used to test the magazines for scratches during the camera prep.

dutch angle   A camera angle in which the camera is tilted either left or right so that the image will appear diagonally within the frame.

dutch head   A special type of head that is usually attached to the standard fluid head and that allows the shooting of "dutch-angle" shots. It is set up so that the tilt action is opposite from the tilt of the regular head and so gives the effect of the dutch angle.

duvetyne   Black cloth that is most often used to cover windows on a location to prevent any light from entering the set. It may be used for many other things, including covering the camera, the operator, and the assistant if their reflections are seen in a particular shot. When shooting into a window or reflective surface, the camera and all people around it must be covered in black so that they are not seen in the shot.

Eastman, George The inventor of standard 35mm motion picture film and founder of Eastman Kodak Company.

Eastman Kodak (Kodak) Trade name of a brand of professional motion picture film stock.

Eclair The trade name of a brand of 16mm and 35mm motion picture camera manufactured by Eclair International in France. The most commonly used Eclair cameras include the ACL and NPR in 16mm.

ECU See *extreme close-up*.

EI See *exposure index*.

8mm The narrow film gauge that was introduced in 1932 and intended primarily for home-movie use. In the mid-1960s, Super 8 film was introduced to replace 8mm; 8mm film is no longer available. Most people now use some type of video camera or camcorder for home movies.

80A filter A blue conversion filter that is used to convert daylight-balanced film for filming with tungsten-light sources. It requires an exposure compensation of two stops.

85 filter An orange conversion filter used to convert tungsten-balanced film for filming under daylight conditions. It requires an exposure compensation of two-thirds stop.

ELS See *extreme long shot*.

emulsion One of the three components that make up any piece of film stock (Figure A.2). It is the light-sensitive part of the film stock and the place where the photographic image is recorded. Emulsion is made up of particles of silver halide suspended in gelatin. Exposure to light causes a change in the silver halide crystals and forms what is called a latent image on the film. When treated with certain chemicals in the developing and printing process at the lab, a visual image is formed.

end slate   See *tail slate.*

enhancing filter   A filter used to improve the color saturation of red and orange objects in the scene while having very little effect on other colors. It usually requires an exposure compensation of one and one-half to two stops.

episode   Term usually used to refer to the weekly segment of a particular television series. Each week a different story line is covered on the show. The standard number of episodes for a television series is usually 22 to 26.

establishing shot   A long shot or wide shot that is usually at the beginning of a filmed sequence and establishes the location and setting for the scene. It also helps to set the mood for the scene.

expendables   Items such as tape, pens, markers, batteries, and so on, that are used by the camera department in the daily performance of the job. They are called *expendables* because they are usually used up during the course of a production.

exposed film   Any film that has been run through the camera and contains a photographed image. Exposed film must be kept in a cool dark place and opened in a darkroom only.

exposure   The f-stop that has been set for a particular shot; also, the subjecting of film to light. The degree of exposure is determined by how much light strikes the film and how much time the light is allowed to strike the film.

exposure index (EI)   A numeric value assigned to a film stock that is a measurement of the film's speed, or sensitivity to light. The higher the number, the faster the film and the more sensitive it is to light. It may be used in the same way as the ASA number or DIN number. See also *ASA number; DIN number.*

exposure meter   A device that measures the amount or intensity of light falling on a scene. The two main types of exposure meters are reflected and incident. A reflected meter measures the amount of light reflected from a subject; a spot meter is one type of reflected light meter. An incident meter measures the amount of light falling on a subject. See also *incident meter; light meter; spot meter.*

exposure time   The amount of time that each frame of film is exposed to light. For normal motion picture photography, the standard exposure time is 1/50th of a second with a film speed of 24 frames per second.

EXT   See *exterior scene.*

exterior scene (EXT)   Any filmed scene that takes place outdoors.

extra   An actor or actress appearing in the background or crowd sequences of a scene. Extras help to make the scenes look more realistic and usually do not have any lines or perform any special business that would separate them from other extras.

extreme close-up (ECU)   A very tight close-up shot that shows much detail. On an actor, it may be a shot of the eyes reacting or a shot of the mouth. It is used many times for a specific dramatic effect.

extreme long shot (ELS)   A wide-angle shot showing a view of a large area. It is usually shot from a great distance and often from high above the area being filmed.

eyebrow   A small flag that mounts directly to the matte box and is used to block any light from hitting the lens (Figures E.1, E.2). It may also be called a *sunshade*. See also *french flag; lens shade; sunshade.*

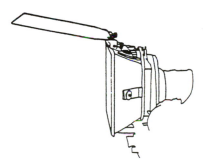

Figure E.1   Arriflex matte box with eyebrow attached. (Reprinted from *The ARRI 35 Book*, with permission of the Arriflex Corporation.)

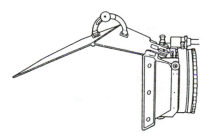

Figure E.2   Panavision matte box with eyebrow attached. (Courtesy of Panavision, Inc.)

eyelight A light that is placed in such a way as to produce a sparkle or highlight in the actor's eyes. It may be placed to one side of the camera, directly over the camera, or even on the camera itself. When placed on the camera, it is sometimes referred to as an *obie light*. See also *obie light*.

eyeline The line of vision of an actor relative to the camera. The eyeline of the performer takes into consideration not only the left and right direction of the look but also the correct height of the look. When filming, it is a good idea to keep unnecessary objects out of the actor's eyeline to make it easier for the actor to concentrate on his or her performance. The script supervisor must watch the actor's eyelines from shot to shot so that the continuity of the scene is maintained. The actor must be looking in the same direction for all coverage shots of a particular scene.

Eyemo Trade name of a small compact 35mm camera manufactured by the Bell & Howell Company. Eyemo cameras are often used when filming stunts or action scenes where many cameras are needed. They are usually placed in some type of protective housing and operated by remote control. Because of the small size, they are often placed inside of cars for filming certain stunt or point-of-view shots. They can only film with a 100-foot daylight spool, which lasts approximately one minute at normal sync speed.

eyepiece The attachment on the camera that allows the camera operator to view the scene as it is being filmed (Figures E.3, E.4). On most modern film cameras, a mirror shutter directs the image entering the lens to the eyepiece for the operator to view. The eyepiece usually contains an adjustable diopter to compensate for the differences in each person's vision and some type of rubber eyecup for comfort and for protection of the operator's eye. On some cameras, there are three lengths of eyepieces available, short, medium, and long. See also *viewfinder*.

Figure E.3 Panavision long eyepiece. (Courtesy of Panavision, Inc.)

Figure E.4   Panavision short eyepiece. (Courtesy of Panavision, Inc.)

eyepiece cover   A small round cover, with a hole in the center, usually made of foam or chamois material and placed on the eyepiece to make it more comfortable for the camera operator.

eyepiece extension   A long version of the camera eyepiece (Figure E.3); used when a short eyepiece is not convenient or comfortable for the camera operator. It is used most often when the camera is mounted to a geared head.

eyepiece heater   Also called **eyepiece warmer**. A heater element used to keep the eyepiece warm when shooting in cold weather situations. It prevents the eyepiece from fogging.

eyepiece leveler   A long adjustable rod that is used to keep the eyepiece level while the camera is panning and tilting. The eyepiece leveler allows the eyepiece to remain at a comfortable position for the camera operator when doing extreme tilt moves with the camera.

eyepiece warmer   See *eyepiece heater*.

feature film   A motion picture that is intended for distribution to movie theaters. It is usually 1 1/2 to 2 hours in length.

feed side   The side of the magazine that contains the fresh, unexposed film. On some magazines, the feed side is separate from the take-up side (Figure C.11), while on other magazines the feed and take-up sides may be contained in the same compartment (Figure D.8).

field of view   See *angle of view.*

fill light   A light that is used to fill in or remove the shadows that are cast by the main light source of the scene.

film can   A metal or plastic container in which the fresh, raw stock is packaged. Any exposed film or short ends created during shooting, after being placed in a black bag, can be stored in a film can. A roll of film should never be placed in a film can without first being placed in a black bag. See also *black bag.*

film plane   The point located behind the lens where the film is held in place during exposure. It is the plane where the rays of light entering the lens come together in sharp focus. See also *focal plane.*

film speed   The rating assigned to a film based on its sensitivity to light. Slow-speed film is not very sensitive to light, and high-speed film is very sensitive to light. The film speed is expressed as *ASA, DIN,* or *EI* numbers.

film-to-video synchronizer   A device used when filming a video monitor image with a film camera (Figure F.1). Because the standard frame rate of video is different from that of film, the synchronizer must be used between the camera and the video source. The film-to-video synchronizer eliminates the moving bars on the screen, which are common when filming a video image without using any kind of synchro-

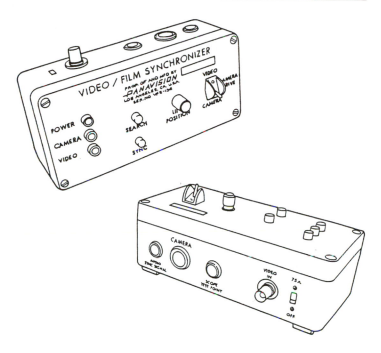

Figure F.1   Film-to-video synchronizer. (Courtesy of Panavsion, Inc.)

nizer. When this unit is used, the camera shutter must be adjusted to 144 degrees when filming at standard 24 fps.

filter   A piece of optically correct glass or gel that is placed in front of a lens or light source to cause a change in the image or a change in the light. The filter may be a special color or have a particular texture that gives the desired effect.

filter pouch   A padded case that is available in the same size as any filter. It is used to store and protect the filter when it is not in place on the camera.

filter trays   Compartments used to hold a filter in the matte box. The trays usually slide in and out of the matte box and come in various sizes to accommodate different filter sizes.

fine cut   A refined version of the edited rough cut of the film. It usually approximates the length of the final version of the film.

1st AC   See *first camera assistant.*

1st AD   See *first assistant director.*

first assistant director (1st AD)   The director's assistant, who keeps things running smoothly on the set. The 1st AD determines the call times for cast and crew. Before each shot, the 1st AD calls for quiet on the set and instructs the sound mixer and camera operator to roll sound and camera. Before production starts, he or she reads the script and breaks it down for scheduling. The 1st AD determines which scenes will be filmed each day, in what order they will be filmed, and the number of extras needed and coordinates with other departments of the film crew to be sure that everything is set for each filming day.

first camera assistant (1st AC)   A member of the camera crew whose duties include setting up and maintaining the camera, changing lenses and filters, loading film into the camera, keeping the camera in working order and maintaining focus during shooting. The 1st AC works very closely with the director of photography and the camera operator during filming.

Fisher   Trade name for a brand of camera dolly (Figure D.10).

fish-eye lens   An extreme wide-angle lens that gives a very distorted view of the scene.

fixed-focus lens   A nonadjustable lens that focuses at a fixed distance from the film plane. In most cases, a fixed-focus lens is a wide-angle lens.

flare   A bright spot or flash of light in the photographic image. It may be caused by lights shining directly into the lens or by reflections from shiny surfaces.

flat rate   A fixed, unchanging fee paid to an actor or technician for their services. It is different from an hourly or daily rate because there is no overtime paid. Some producers will try to pay only a flat rate so that they can save money by making the crew work longer hours with no additional compensation.

FLB filter   A filter that is used when shooting under fluorescent lights with indoor-type-B films. It requires an exposure compensation of one stop.

FLD filter   A filter that is used when filming under fluorescent lights with daylight-type film. It requires an exposure compensation of one stop.

fluid head   A camera-mounting platform that allows the camera operator to do smooth pan and tilt moves during shooting. Its internal elements contain a highly viscous fluid that controls the amount of tension on the pan and tilt parts of the head. It is attached to a high hat, tripod, or dolly and is usually operated by using one or two handles that are mounted

Figure F.2   O'Connor Model 100C fluid head. (Courtesy of O'Connor Camera Support Systems.)

to the sides of the head (Figures F.2–F.4). See also *friction head; geared head*.

foamtip swab   A long wooden or plastic stick that contains a small foam swab on one end; similar to a cotton swab. It may be used to remove any excess oil when oiling the camera. See also *cotton swab*.

focal length   The distance between the optical center of the lens and the film plane when the lens is focused at infinity. Different lenses are referred to by their focal lengths, which are usually expressed in millimeters, such as 25mm, 32mm, 50mm, and so on. A short-focal-length lens has a wide angle of view, and a long-focal-length, or telephoto, lens has a narrow angle of view.

focal plane   The specific point behind the lens where the image is focused onto the piece of film. As the film travels through the camera, it is held between the pressure plate and the aperture plate in the film gate. This area, where it is held while the image is being recorded, is the focal plane. See also *film plane*.

focal plane shutter   A rotating shutter located at the focal plane that alternately blocks light from striking the film and then allows the light to strike the film. It works along with the mirror shutter of the camera. When the shutter is open, light strikes the film, forming an image.

Figure F.3   Sachtler Studio II fluid head. (Courtesy of Sachtler Corporation.)

Figure F.4   Sachtler fluid head mounted on standard tripod and spreader. (Courtesy of Sachtler Corporation.)

When the shutter is closed, no light strikes the film, and the film is being transported through the camera bringing the next frame into position.

focus   The point in the scene that appears sharp and clear when viewed through the camera eyepiece. Also, the act of adjusting the lens to produce a sharp image. Any image that is sharp and well defined is called "in focus," and an image that appears soft or fuzzy is called "out of focus." Focus may be determined by looking through the eyepiece and turning the focus barrel of the lens until the image appears sharp. It also may be determined by measuring the distance from the film plane to the object being photographed.

focus chart   A special chart that is used when testing photographic lenses (Figure F.5). It is used to determine if the lens focus is accurate according to the markings on the side of the lens. While performing the camera prep, the first camera assistant, using a tape measure, places the chart at various distances from the camera and looks through the camera and adjusts the focus barrel of the lens so that the image is sharp. The 1st AC then checks the focus markings on the lens to see if the eye-focused distance matches the measured distance.

focus extension   Accessory for the follow focus mechanism, which makes the job of focusing easier. The focus extension attaches to the right side of the follow focus so focus can be pulled from either side of the camera. A flexible focus accessory may be attached to either side of the follow focus mechanism. This flexible piece is sometimes called a *focus whip* or a *whip* (Figure W.1).

focus puller   A camera-crew member who is responsible for maintaining focus during a shot. During the rehearsal, measurements are taken to various points on the set. During shooting, the focus puller adjusts the focus barrel of the lens so that the image will remain in focus throughout the shot. In the United States, the focus puller is usually the same as the first camera assistant.

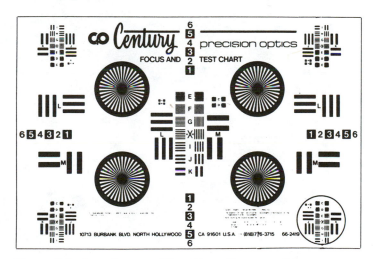

Figure F.5   Lens Focus and Test Chart. (Courtesy of Century Precision Optics.)

focus whip   See *whip*.

follow focus (following focus)   Also called **pulling focus**. The act of turning the focus barrel of the lens during the shot so that the actors stay in focus as they move through the scene. When following focus, it is important to know the depth of field for the shot.

follow focus mechanism   A geared attachment that mounts to the camera and contains gears that are engaged to teeth on the lens (Figures F.6, F.7). It enables the first camera assistant to follow focus, or pull focus, during the shot.

fog filter   A filter that simulates the effect of natural fog. A fog filter will cause any light in the shot to have a flare. No exposure compensation is required.

footage counter   A digital or dial type of gauge on the camera that shows the amount of film that has been run through the camera (Figure F.8, F.9). Each time the camera is loaded with a fresh roll of film, the first camera assistant should reset the footage counter to zero.

footcandle   A unit of measurement for determining the intensity of light. It is derived from the amount of light emitted by a standard candle at a distance of 1 foot.

Figure F.6   Arriflex studio follow focus mechanism. (Photo courtesy of the Arriflex Corporation.)

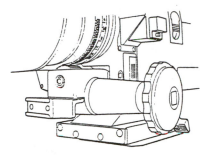

Figure F.7 Panavision standard follow focus mechanism. (Courtesy of Panavision, Inc.)

meter/feet

FOOTAGE
COUNTER

TACHOMETER

f/sec.   reset

read

Figure F.8 ARRIFLEX 35-3 digital display showing footage counter and tachometer. (Photo courtesy of the Arriflex Corporation.)

forced call Requiring a member of the cast or crew to report to work, without having a minimum amount of time off since completing work the previous day. It is not done very often because the producer must pay an additional amount of money to the person receiving the forced call. The minimum time off required between one day and the next is usually between 10 and 12 hours.

format See *aspect ratio.*

format The film gauge being shot—16mm, 35mm, or 65mm.

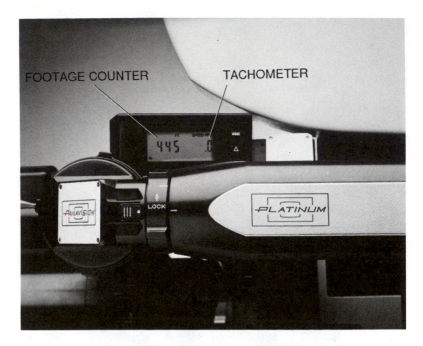

Figure F.9 Panavision Platinum digital display showing footage counter and tachometer. (Courtesy of Panavision, Inc.)

four-inch lens (4-inch lens) A slang term used in the early days of filmmaking to indicate a 100mm lens. The term is still used today by some cameramen.

fps See *frames per second.*

frame An individual image on a piece of film. Each individual frame contains specific elements that make up a shot. The film consists of many frames that, when projected at sync speed of 24 frames per second, give the illusion of motion.

frame rate The speed at which the film runs through the camera. It is expressed in terms of frames per second (fps).

frames per second (fps) The standard measurement for film speed as it runs through the camera or projector. The standard film speed rate in the United States when filming with synchronous sound recording is 24 fps.

freelance   A worker who is not a staff employee of a company. Payment for services is received after submission of an invoice or a time card to the company. See also *independent contractor*.

french flag   A small flag that is mounted onto the camera and used to help keep any lights from causing a flare in the lens. It consists of a flexible arm onto which the small flag is attached. The arm is positioned so that the flag keeps the flare from striking the front element of the lens (Figure F.10). See also *eyebrow*.

friction head   A camera-mounting platform that allows the camera operator to perform smooth pan and tilt moves when composing the scene. Its internal elements create friction by rubbing against each other, creating the tension for the pan and tilt portions of the head. It may be mounted to a high hat, tripod, or dolly for use during filming. See also *fluid head; geared head*.

Fries Engineering   Trade name of a manufacturer of motion picture equipment including the *Mitchell Fries 35mm Camera* and *Fries Filters*.

front box   A wooden box that attaches to the front of the camera head and is used to hold a variety of tools and accessories (Figure F.11). It is mainly used by the first camera assistant for storing the tape measure,

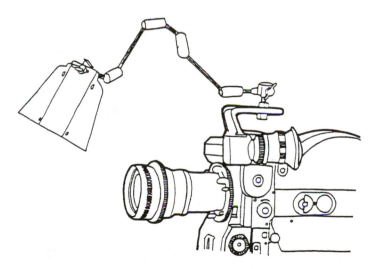

Figure F.10   French flag mounted for Arriflex 16SR. (Reprinted from *The 16SR Book*, with permission of the Arriflex Corporation.)

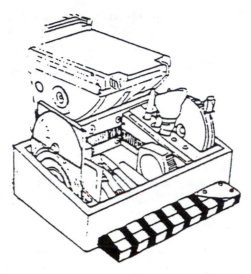

Figure F.11   Front box mounted to Arriflex geared head. (Reprinted from *The ARRI 35 Book*, with permission of the Arriflex Corporation.)

miniflashlight, depth-of-field charts, pens, permanent felt markers, compressed air, gum, mints, and so on. The director of photography may also use it as a place to keep meters during filming.

f-stop   The setting on the lens that corresponds to the size of the aperture (Figure F.12). It is an indication of the amount of light entering the lens and does not take into account any light loss due to absorption. The

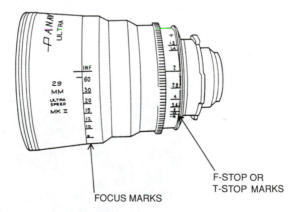

FOCUS MARKS

F-STOP OR T-STOP MARKS

Figure F.12   Panavision lens showing focus marks, f-stop or t-stop marks. (Courtesy of Panavision, Inc.)

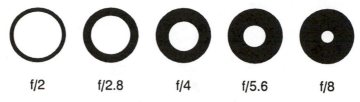

f/2   f/2.8   f/4   f/5.6   f/8

Figure F.13   Diaphragm openings for various f-stop openings. (Not drawn to scale.)

f-stop of a lens is determined by dividing the focal length of the lens by the diameter of the aperture opening. The smaller the number, the larger the opening (Figure F.13). The standard series of f-stop numbers is 1, 1.4, 2, 2.8, 4, 5.6, 8, 11, 16, 22, 32, and so on. Each f-stop opening admits half the amount of light as the stop before it.

Fuji   Trade name for a brand of professional motion picture film stock.

full aperture   The entire area of the film frame, which extends out to the perforations on the film. When looking through the eyepiece, it extends beyond the frame lines inscribed on the ground glass.

full shot   A shot that shows the actor from head to toe. A full shot is not the same as a wide shot.

G See *good*.

gaffer The member of the film crew who is the chief electrician or lighting technician. The gaffer is responsible for lighting the set, based on instructions received from the director of photography, and instructs the lighting crew where to place lights before and during shooting.

gaffer tape Cloth tape, usually 2 inches wide, that may be used to tape up any holes or cracks in the darkroom; also used for any taping job that requires tape wider than the 1-inch-wide camera tape. It is available in many colors, including gray, black, and white.

G & M Products Manufacturer of a brand of motion picture camera batteries.

gate The part of the camera where the film is held while it is being exposed. Sometimes *gate* means the opening that is cut into the aperture plate and allows light to strike the film and create an exposure on the film. Sometimes the aperture plate, pressure plate, pulldown claw, and registration pin are included in a reference to the gate. During filming, after each printed take, the gate must be checked to be sure that it is clear of any pieces of film emulsion, or hairs, that may show up in the finished film as large ropes in the frame.

geared head A camera-mounting platform that allows the camera operator to do smooth pan and tilt moves during shooting. It may be mounted to a high hat, tripod, or dolly and is operated by turning two control wheels that are connected to gears in the head. One control wheel is mounted on the left side and is used for panning the camera. The other control wheel is mounted toward the back of the head and is used for making any tilt moves (Figures G.1, G.2). See also *fluid head; friction head*.

gel A plastic-type material, available in many shades and colors, that is used to alter the effect of a light source. The gel may be placed directly in

Figure G.1   Arriflex ARRIHEAD geared head. (Photo courtesy of the Arriflex Corporation.)

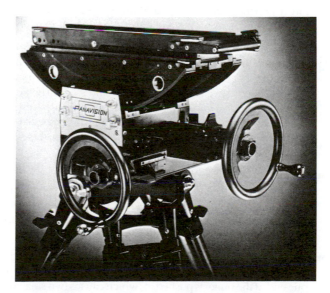

Figure G.2   Panavision Panahead geared head. (Courtesy of Panavision, Inc.)

front of the light, or it may be placed in front of or behind the lens to alter the image recorded on the film.

George Eastman   See *Eastman, George*.

good (G)   Any take that the director chooses as his preference for each scene. These takes are circled on the camera report. It may also refer to the total amount of footage for all takes on the camera report that are circled and are to be printed or transferred by the lab.

gopher   See *production assistant*.

graduated filter, grad filter   A filter that is of variable density so that one half of it is clear and the other half contains the filter. Some of the most common graduated filters are the graduated neutral density filters and color graduated filters.

grain   The texture of the film image, which is caused by particles of silver halide that make up the emulsion part of the film stock. The faster the film (higher ASA) the more grain will be visible.

gray scale (gray card)   A standard series of tonal shades ranging from white to grey to black. The card or scale may be photographed at the beginning of each film roll and is used by the lab when processing the film to check for the correct tonal values in the film.

grease pencils   Erasable crayon-like pencils used for making focus marks directly on the lens or focus-marking disk. Some of the colors in which they are available are white, yellow, red, and black. One popular brand of grease pencils is the Stabilo brand.

grip   A member of the film crew who performs much of the manual labor needed on the set. A grip helps to move set pieces, sets lighting control devices, builds special camera mounts, and so on. The key grip is the supervisor of the grip department. A dolly grip is responsible for making dolly and crane moves and for setting up special dolly tracks for these moves. A grip would be equivalent to a stage hand in the theater. See also *dolly grip; key grip*.

ground glass   A small piece of optical material onto which a portion of the light from the lens is focused allowing the camera operator to see the image that the lens is seeing. It is usually inscribed with lines to indicate the edges of the frame, which assists the operator in composing the shot (Figure C.16).

ground glass puller   Spring-activated clamp device that is used to remove the ground glass from many motion picture cameras. The plunger on one end of the puller is pushed in, which causes two small wire prongs to protrude from the opposite end. By grasping the ground glass with the wire prongs and releasing the plunger, the ground glass is held securely and may be pulled from the camera.

Guild Kelly Calculator   Trade name for a brand of depth-of-field calculator used by many 1st ACs.

hair   A very fine piece of emulsion that appears in the gate and can look like an actual hair. If not removed from the gate, it will appear as a large rope on a big movie screen. It may be caused by the emulsion being scraped off the film as it travels through the gate. There may be a small burr in the metal of the aperture plate that would cause the emulsion to be removed as the film travels through the camera.

hairlight   A light that is placed behind an actor to highlight the hair and separate it from the background in the scene. A hairlight may also be referred to as a *backlight*. It sometimes creates a silhouette or halo effect. See also *backlight*.

hand-held shot   Any shot that is done with the camera physically held on the camera operator's shoulder during filming. It is often used for point-of-view shots of an actor walking or moving through the scene. When filming hand-held shots, it is usually customary to have a wide-angle lens on the camera, which helps to minimize the shakiness associated within many hand-held-camera shots. Smaller magazines should be ordered, along with the left- and right-hand grips and a shoulder pad, if any hand-held shots are to be done. The smaller magazines reduce the weight of the camera, making it easier for the operator to carry the camera during filming (Figures C.4, C.5). See also *camera, hand-held*.

hand-held accessories   Any item needed to make hand-held shots easier. These items may include left- and right-hand grips, a shoulder pad, a smaller clamp-on-style matte box, and smaller film magazines. A hand-held shot requires that the camera be held on the camera operator's shoulder, so the hand grips are used to make the camera easier to hold, and the shoulder pad makes it more comfortable.

hand-held camera   See *camera, hand-held*.

hard mattes   Covers that are placed in front of the matte box to block any unwanted light from striking the lens (Figure H.1a). They have the

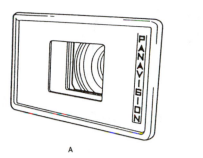 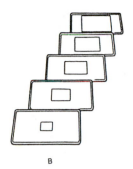

A   B

Figure H.1   Matte-box hard mattes. (a) Hard matte mounted on matte box. (b) Set of hard mattes. (Courtesy of Panavision, Inc.)

center portion cut out in various sizes depending on the focal length of the lens being used (Figure H.1b).

Harrison & Harrison   Trade name of a brand of motion picture camera filters.

head   A camera-mounting platform that allows the camera operator to make smooth pan and tilt moves during the shot. A head may be one of three types: fluid, friction or geared. The two most commonly used heads are fluid heads and geared heads (Figures F.2–F.4, G.1, G.2). See also *fluid head; friction head; geared head.*

head room   The area in the film frame above the actor's head. Head room is considered too much when the actor's eyes are below the center of the frame, and too little when the top of the actor's head is cut off by the top frame line. Too much head room or too little head room can make the frame look unbalanced unless there is some specific reason for composing the shot that way.

head slate   A slate that is photographed at the beginning of a shot. When doing a head slate, the slate is held right side up.

hiatus   A scheduled vacation or planned interruption in the filming schedule. Usually when filming a television series, the production company works for 9 or 10 months and then shuts down for the remainder of the year until they are ready to start filming a new year's episodes.

high angle   A shot that is done with the camera placed very high above the action and pointed down toward the subject or action. When doing a high-angle shot, the camera may be placed on a tripod, on a ladder, or even on a crane boom arm.

high hat (hi hat)   A very low camera mount used when filming low-angle shots (Figure H.2). The head is mounted to the high hat, and then the camera is mounted onto the head.

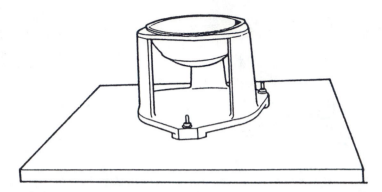

Figure H.2   High hat.

high speed   Any filmed shot that is done at a speed greater than normal sync speed of 24 fps. There are many specialized cameras that allow filming at high speeds anywhere from 300 to 2000 fps. When filming at high speed, the final projected film image will have the illusion of moving at a much slower rate of speed. It is very useful for slowing down fast action.

Hirschmann Forceps   Trade name of a brand of ground glass puller. See also *ground glass puller.*

HMI   An acronym that comes from Hg, the symbol for mercury; M for medium arc; and I for iodides. An HMI light is one which has a color temperature which is equal to the color temperature of daylight. See also *HMI lights.*

HMI lights   Lighting devices that produce a color temperature equivalent to the color temperature of natural daylight. They are often used when filming daylight interior scenes to help supplement the existing day-light coming through the windows. Because they are powered from a ballast, they will cause a flicker in the photographic image if the camera is not run at the proper speed. There are tables available that list the correct speeds to use when filming with HMI lights.

HMI speed control   A speed control used when filming with HMI lights. HMI lights are balanced for daylight, and they can only be used when filming at certain speeds or there will be a flicker in the photographic image.

honeywagon   A large mobile truck or trailer that contains dressing rooms for the cast and rest-room facilities for the cast and crew.

hot set   Any set that has been completely dressed with furniture, props, lighting, and so on, and is ready for shooting or is still being used for shooting. Usually a sign reading "HOT SET" is placed on or near the set to warn the cast and crew not to disturb or touch anything on the set.

hyperfocal distance   The closest point in front of the lens that is in acceptable sharp focus when the lens is focused at infinity. This distance is determined by the focal length of the lens and the f-stop setting on the lens. If the focus of the lens is set to the hyperfocal distance, everything from one-half the distance to infinity will be in focus.

IATSE   See *International Alliance of Theatrical and Stage Employees.*

incident light   All the light that falls on the subject being filmed. To measure the amount of incident light falling on a subject, an incident meter is used. See also *incident meter.*

incident meter   A light meter used to measure the amount of incident light that is falling on a subject (Figures I.1, I.2). The incident meter usually contains a white translucent dome, which is called a *photosphere.* The photosphere simulates a three-dimensional shape (such as a face). Incident light comes from many sources around a subject, and the photosphere helps to average the amount of light falling on the subject from these sources. See also *exposure meter; incident light; light meter.*

independent contractor   A film technician who is hired by the production company to perform a specific job on a production. The independent contractor usually works on a freelance basis and not as a contract employee. At the completion of services, the independent contractor usually submits an invoice to the production company for payment of services rendered. See also *freelance.*

independent production   A film production that is not financed by a major studio. It is usually financed by a single person or a group of people. Most independent productions do not have name actors, and the crew is usually smaller and not as experienced as the crew on a bigger-budget union production. The producers may not have enough money to produce the blockbuster, big-budget films associated with most major studios or production companies. Many small independent productions have been released by major studios and have gone on to become huge successes.

insert shot (insert)   A close-up or extreme close-up shot that is inserted into a filmed sequence to show a particular point of detail. A hand

Figure I.2 SPECTRA
PROFESSIONAL incident
light meter. (Courtesy of
Spectra Cine, Inc.)

Figure I.1 Minolta Auto Meter
III incident light meter. (Courtesy
of Minolta Corporation.)

reaching into a drawer or a close-up of a photograph at which
someone is looking may be insert shots.

insert slate A small-scene slate used to identify any MOS or insert shots
being filmed. The information written on it includes the production
title, roll number, scene and take numbers, date, director's name, and
director of photography's name (Figure I.3). The insert slate is different
from the sync slate because it usually does not contain the clap sticks.

INT See *interior scene*.

interior scene (INT) Any filmed scene that takes place indoors.

intermittent movement The starting and stopping movement of the film
transport mechanism as it advances the film through the camera. To the
human eye, it appears that the film going through the motion picture
camera is moving continuously. In reality, each frame stops long
enough in the film gate so that it may be exposed and then is moved
out of the way so the next frame may be exposed.

DATE	UNIT	CAMERA
SCENE	TAKE	ROLL
CAMERAMAN		PROD. NO.

Figure I.3   Insert slate.

International Alliance of Theatrical and Stage Employees (IATSE)
The name of the parent organization of over 1000 local unions in North America. The IA, as it is sometimes called, has local branches that represent members working in all areas of film production and also represent workers in the distribution and exhibition areas of the film industry. The union sets the working conditions, wages, and so on, for all employees under its jurisdiction.

iris   An adjustable diaphragm that is used to control the amount of light that is transmitted through the lens and exposes the film. The iris of the lens consists of overlapping leaves that form a circular opening to vary the amount of light coming through the lens. Changing the f-stop or t-stop setting of the lens changes the iris opening of the lens. See also *diaphragm*.

iris rods   Metal rods of varying lengths that are used to support the matte box, follow focus, lens support, and other accessories on the camera. Each time a different lens is placed on the camera, the rods must be changed or adjusted so that the matte box and accessories will fit properly against the lens.

juicer Slang term used to refer to any electrician working on a film set.

jump cut An editing cut between scenes or within a scene in which the action or placement of objects changes abruptly. It is achieved by either taking out a section of the scene or by stopping the camera and then moving it in closer without changing the camera angle. This type of editing has traditionally been regarded as unacceptable filmmaking, but some of the newer filmmakers use this technique to achieve a desired effect. It is sometimes used as a means of compressing time within a scene.

K   See *Kelvin*.

Kelvin (K)   A unit for measuring heat; 0 K equals -273.15 °C. Color temperature is measured in degrees Kelvin.

key grip   The head of the grip department who supervises the grips in the placement of lighting control devices. The key grip works closely with the director of photography and the gaffer. See also *director of photography; gaffer; grip*.

key light   A light that is used as the main light source for the scene. It is the principal and dominant lighting source for a scene and is usually the first light placed in position by the director of photography. The remaining lights for the scene are then placed according to the position of the key light.

kicker   A light that may be used to highlight a specific area of the scene. It may be used to bring attention to a particular object in the scene. A kicker is often used to add a sparkle to the actor's eyes and would then be called an eyelight. See also *eyelight*.

Kimwipes   Soft tissuelike material similar to lens tissue. They can be used for cleaning filters or any other small cleaning job but should not be used to clean lenses.

kinetograph   The first motion picture camera, which was developed by Thomas Edison and W. K. L. Dickson in 1888. It was first used in 1889 and patented in 1891.

kinetoscope   A device used to view the filmed images that were made with the kinetograph. It was invented in 1889 by Thomas Edison and W. K. L. Dickson and patented in 1891.

kit rental   See *box rental*.

Kodak   See *Eastman Kodak*.

lab   The facility where the film is sent to be processed, developed, and printed.

latitude   The ability of the film emulsion to be underexposed or overexposed and still produce an acceptable image. Many of the newer, faster-speed films have a greater latitude than the earlier slow-speed films.

leading space   The open space in the frame from the front edge of an object to the edge of the frame; space in the direction that an actor is looking or that something in the frame is moving. It is generally not acceptable to frame an actor with his or her nose right against the edge of the frame or perfectly in the center of the frame. If the actor is looking to the left, there should be more space on the left of the frame; and if looking to the right, there should be more space on the right of the frame. The same idea applies to a moving object. It should not be in the center of the frame while filming. It is better to "lead" it and keep some space on the side of the frame in the direction that it is moving. This method of composing shots is much more appealing to the viewer, allowing for better enjoyment of the film.

left-hand grip   An attachment for the camera used when shooting handheld shots. It is placed on the left side of the camera and allows the camera operator to hold the camera steady in a comfortable position for shooting.

legs   A slang term used to refer to the tripod for the camera. *Baby legs* refers to the smaller tripod, and *standard legs* refers to the larger tripod (Figure B.1).

lens   An optical device through which light rays pass to form a focused image on a piece of film. Lenses are usually referred to by their focal length. There are basically two main types of lenses used for motion picture photography: prime and zoom. Prime lenses are lenses of a single, fixed, focal length such as 25mm, 35mm, 50mm, and so on. A zoom lens is a lens of variable focal length; the lens moves in and out, thus changing its focal length, by turning the barrel of the lens. The zoom is usually referred to by its range of focal lengths, such as 10mm to 100mm, 20mm to 100mm, 25mm to 250mm, and so on. A type of prime lens that is also available is the telephoto lens. It is a lens of an extremely long focal length such as 200mm, 300mm, 400mm, 600mm, and so on. Telephoto lenses allow you to film close-up shots of objects that are very far away (Figures L.1, L.2).

Figure L.1 Carl Zeiss/ARRIFLEX lenses. (Photo courtesy of the Arriflex Corporation.)

Figure L.2 Panavision Ultra Speed lenses. (Courtesy of Panavision, Inc.)

lens cleaner   A liquid that is used, along with lens tissue, to clean lenses and filters. Lens cleaner should be used to clean lenses only when absolutely necessary. Professional motion picture lenses have a coating on the front element, and too much cleaning with the lens cleaner can wear down this coating. See also *lens tissue.*

lens extender   An attachment that is mounted between the lens and the camera to increase the focal length of the lens being used. The most common lens extenders are the 1.4x, which increases the focal length by 1.4 times the actual focal length, and the 2x, which doubles the actual focal length. When a lens extender is used, the exposure must be adjusted by the strength of the extender, for example, for a 2x extender, the exposure is adjusted by two stops.

lens light   Also called **little light; niner light**. A small light, mounted to a flexible arm, that is attached to the camera and allows the first camera assistant to see the lens focus and zoom markings when filming in a dark set.

lens shade   A rubber or metal device that either screws onto or is clamped onto the front of the lens. It is used to hold round filters and to keep any stray light from striking the front element of the lens. See also *sunshade.*

lens speed   The widest f-stop to which the lens opens. The smaller the f-number, which means the larger the opening of the lens aperture, then the faster the lens. Fast lenses allow filming in very low light situations.

lens tissue   Small tissues, along with lens cleaner, used to clean lenses and filters. It is recommended that a dry piece of lens tissue never be used on a lens because it may scratch the coating or front element of the lens. See also *lens cleaner.*

lens turret   A rotating device on the front of the camera onto which more than one lens may be mounted. By rotating the turret, the cameraman may choose the lens with which to film. Lens turrets were very common on the earlier cameras and are not found today on the newer film cameras.

L-handle   See *speed crank.*

light meter   A device that is used to measure the amount of light illuminating a scene. An incident meter would be used to measure the amount of light falling on a subject, that is, the incident light. A spot meter would be used to measure the light being emitted by a subject, that is, the reflected light. The light meter is calibrated in such a way so that the measurements are expressed in f-stops for a given film speed and exposure time. See also *exposure meter; incident meter; spot meter.*

line of vision   See *eyeline.*

little light   See *lens light*.

LLD filter   A filter used when filming with tungsten-balanced film in low-light daylight situations. It requires no exposure compensation.

loader   The member of the camera crew who is responsible for loading and unloading the film into the magazines. A loader is usually used on larger productions when two or more cameras are being used.

location   Any locale used for filming that is away from the studio or production company. When filming on location, the production company must provide food and shelter for the cast and crew. Location filming is used to add authenticity to a film that may not be achieved by filming on a studio stage or studio back lot.

lock off   Any shot that is done with the pan and tilt mechanisms of the camera head locked so that the camera does not move during filming. Many times it is used for a stunt or special-effects shot. A lock off shot may be done in three different ways: one may involve the camera being locked at the beginning of the shot and then released part way through; a second may require the operator to pan and tilt for the beginning of the shot and then lock the camera at a certain point in the action; the third requires the camera to be locked off for the entire shot.

long lens   A telephoto lens or a lens that has a focal length longer than that of a normal lens.

long shot (LS)   A shot in which the main subject of the shot usually occupies a small portion of the frame in relation to the overall setting. It is usually filmed with a wide-angle lens, which has a very broad field of view. Long shots do not allow for the viewer to see any great detail in the shot.

loop   A section of film, set to a specific length, that allows for the intermittent movement of the film through the camera during filming. If the loop is not set correctly, the film may become jammed in the camera or magazine, and the camera will not run properly or it may run loudly (Figures L.3–L.5).

lot   The area of land where a studio is located. It includes the offices, dressing rooms, stages, and any other buildings or facilities needed for motion picture production. It may also be used to refer to the back lot area where the building facades are located that are used for exterior filming.

Louma crane   The trade name for a brand of camera crane by which the camera is operated by remote control. The camera is mounted to the special head on the crane, which is connected by a series of cables to a control console containing a video monitor and the pan-and-tilt wheels for the head. By viewing the image on the monitor, the camera

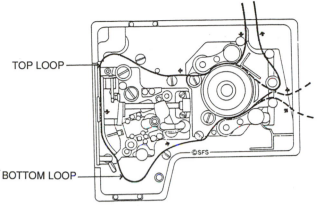

Figure L.3   Threading diagram of Panavision camera showing the top and bottom loops. (Courtesy of Panavision, Inc.)

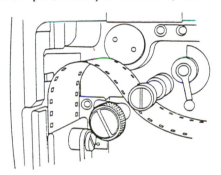

Figure L.4   Close-up view of top loop on Panavision camera. (Courtesy of Panavision, Inc.)

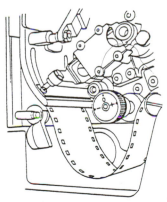

Figure L.5   Close-up view of bottom loop on Panavision camera. (Courtesy of Panavision, Inc.)

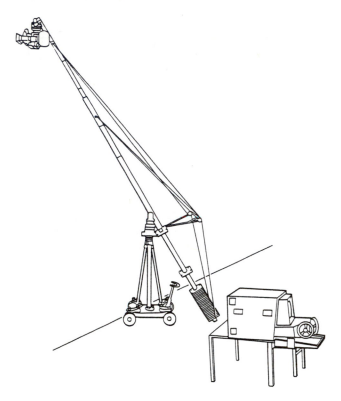

Figure L.6   Louma crane and camera operator remote console. (Courtesy of Panavision, Inc.)

operator is able to compose the shot. The first camera assistant has a separate monitor and a remote control unit that allows for following focus from a distance. The monitor allows the 1st AC to watch the shot and adjust the focus accordingly (Figure L.6).

low-contrast filter (low-con filter)   A filter that lowers the contrast by causing light to spread from highlight areas to shadow areas. It will mute colors, make blacks appear lighter, and also allow more detail in dense-shadow areas. No exposure compensation is required.

low angle   A shot that is done with the camera placed very close to the ground and pointed up toward the subject or action. For a low-angle shot, the camera may be placed directly on the ground or placed on a high hat or on a rocker plate.

macro lens A lens that enables focusing on an object only a few inches away from the lens. Most standard lenses have a close-focusing distance of 4 or 5 feet. A macro lens has a close-focusing distance of 4 or 5 inches.

mag see *magazine.*

magazine (mag) A lightproof container that contains the film before and after exposure. There are two distinct areas in each magazine: the feed side, which contains the fresh unexposed film, and the take-up side, which contains the exposed film. Each time the camera is started, the film travels from the feed side, through the camera, and into the take-up side. Each time the camera is loaded with a new roll of film, a new magazine is attached to the camera (Figures M.1, M.2). The two main types of film magazines are the displacement magazine (Figure D.8) and the coaxial magazine (Figure C.11). See also *coaxial magazine, displacement magazine.*

mag jam See *magazine jam.*

magazine jam (mag jam) The malfunction that happens when the film backs up and becomes piled up in the magazine. This may be caused by torn perforations, causing the film to not engage on the sprockets properly, or by improper threading in the camera or magazine. Improper threading may create a film loop that is too large or too small, causing the camera motor to work harder to move the film through the camera; this extra pressure on the motor may result in the film jamming in the magazine. See also *camera jam.*

Magliner The trade name of a four-wheeled, folding hand truck used by many camera assistants to expedite the moving of the many equipment cases on a film set. Throughout the shooting day, equipment must be moved many times for each different camera setup. By having the cases on the cart, the assistant is saved from having to hand carry each

Figure M.1   Arriflex 35-3 displacement magazines. Front—400 ft. Back—1000 ft. (Photo courtesy of the Arriflex Corporation.)

Figure M.2   Panavision 35mm displacement magazines. Left to right: 250 ft, 500 ft, 1000 ft. (Courtesy of Panavision, Inc.)

case each time it must be moved. The two most common types of Magliner carts are the *Gemini Junior* and the *Gemini Senior.*

mag lite   Small pocket-type flashlight used by most crew people. It has a powerful bulb, and the very bright beam can be adjusted from spotlight to floodlight by turning the head of the light.

mag-lite bulbs   Replacement bulbs for the small flashlight usually used by most camera assistants.

magic hour   The time of day, known as *twilight*, between sundown and darkness. During this time, the light is very warm, and any shadows created are very long. Many scenes are shot during magic hour because of the lighting, to enhance the shot and achieve a certain effect.

marks   Small pieces of colored tape or chalk marks on the ground that are used to identify various positions. They may indicate where the actor is to stand for the shot or where the dolly starts and stops its move, or they may be a reference for focus used by the first camera assistant. When there is more than one actor in a scene, each actor will be assigned a different color mark to avoid any confusion. If the marks are seen in the shot, they will be used for rehearsals and then removed before the scene is shot. Some of the most common types of marks are the box (Figure M.3), T-mark (Figure M.4), toe mark (Figure M.5), and upside-down V (Figure M.6).

martini shot   During filming, the last shot of the day. If it is the last day of filming, it is the last shot of the film. See also *Abby Singer Shot.*

Figure M.3   Example of actor's box mark.

Figure M.4   Example of actor's T-mark.

Figure M.5   Example of actor's toe marks.

Figure M.6   Example of actor's upside-down "V" mark.

master shot   An uninterrupted, overall shot of an entire scene. Usually, one or two master shots are filmed from different camera angles, and then the scene is broken down into segments where the coverage shots are done. Master shots are usually filmed with a wide-angle lens. See also *coverage*.

matte   A special mask with a specified area cut out. When it is placed in front of the lens or in the gate, the area exposed through the cutout is the only area exposed. There are usually separate mattes (called *hard mattes*) for each prime lens being used, and, when placed on the matte box, they help to keep any stray light from striking the lens and causing a lens flare (Figure M8). See also *hard mattes*.

matte box   An accessory that mounts on the front of the camera to shield the lens against unwanted light; also used to hold any filters. It is usually referred to by the size of filters that it normally holds; for example, a matte box that holds 4-by-4-inch filters is called a 4 X 4 matte box (Figures M.7, M.8). In addition to holding two or three square or rectangular filters, most matte boxes have a snap-in piece that holds one round filter, either 4 1/2 inches in diameter or 138mm in diameter. The matte box usually comes with a set of hard mattes for each prime lens being used. Each time a different lens is placed on the camera, the matte box should be adjusted for a proper fit with the lens.

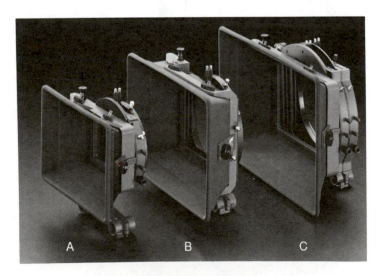

Figure M.7   Arriflex matte boxes. (a) 4 x 4 matte box; (b) 5 x 6 matte box; (c) 6 x 6 matte box. (Courtesy of the Arriflex Corporation.)

Figure M.8   Panavision matte box. (Courtesy of Panavision, Inc.)

MCU   See *medium close-up.*

meal penalty   A monetary amount paid by the production company to the cast and crew whenever they have not been given a meal break after a specified period of time. It is standard to provide a meal break after 6 hours of work. For every half hour or portion of a half hour past the 6 hours, the employee is compensated until the meal break is given.

medium close-up (MCU)   A shot that may be a little too loose to be called a *close-up* but is not wide enough to be called a *medium shot.*

medium long shot (MLS)   A shot that is wider than a medium shot but not as wide as a long shot. The action within the frame is at a position in between the foreground and background of the shot.

medium shot (MS)   A shot that is somewhere between a close-up and a long shot. It usually shows the subject from the waist to the top of the head.

mileage   Also called **drive-to money.** Payment made to the members of the cast and crew to compensate them for driving their own vehicles to a location. This amount is usually paid whenever the distance driven is beyond a specified distance from the production company. See also *studio zone.*

Miller   Trade name of a brand of motion picture camera fluid heads.

minimum call   The minimum number of hours for which an actor or crew member must be paid whether or not the hours are worked.

Minolta   Trade name for a brand of exposure meter (Figures I.1, S.5).

mirrored shutter   A shutter that incorporates a mirror into its design so that the image may be reflected to the viewfinder when the shutter is closed to the film. When the shutter is open, the light goes to the film, and the image is recorded on film. When the shutter is closed, the light strikes the mirror and the image is directed to the viewfinder for the camera operator to view the shot.

Mitchell   A trade name of one of the earlier models of motion picture cameras. It was mainly used for studio work because of its large size. Some of the models of the Mitchell camera include *BNC, BNCR.*

Mitchell Diffusion   The trade name of a brand of motion-picture-camera diffusion filters. As with other diffusion filters, they are used to soften and decrease the sharpness of the image. It is very good for smoothing out facial blemishes or wrinkles. It can also be used for dreamlike effects. When used, this filter may give the appearance that the image is out of focus. Mitchell Diffusion filters are available in various densities from very light to very heavy. They require no exposure compensation.

MLS   See *medium long shot.*

monitor   A television or video screen used by the director during filming to check the framing of the shot and the quality of the performance. It is used in conjunction with a video camera that is attached to the film camera. The video camera sees the same image that the film camera is photographing so that the director can watch the shot during shooting (Figure M9).

monochromatic   Early black and white film in which all colors were rendered as shades of gray. Bright objects would appear white and the darker objects would appear black.

MOS   Any shot that is done without recording synchronous sound. It is an abbreviation that literally means "mit out sound." It was first started by an early director who was of German descent. When doing this type of shot, *MOS* is written on the slate along with the other standard information. When slating a MOS shot, the clap sticks of the slate are usually kept in a closed position.

Moviecam   Trade name for a brand of professional 35mm cameras. The two Moviecam 35mm cameras are the *Superamerica* and the *Compact.*

Figure M.9   Panavision Platinum camera with video assist and monitor. (a) Video assist unit mounted to camera; (b) Video cable; (c) Video monitor. (Courtesy of Panavision, Inc.)

movie of the week (MOW)   A movie that is shown on a weekly basis by one of the major television networks. Each week a different film is shown, usually at the same time and on the same night.

MOW   See *movie of the week.*

MS   See *medium shot.*

multicamera   Any shots that are done by using more than one camera during filming. The different cameras will record the same action of the scene from different angles. Many times, any scenes that contain a great deal of action or dangerous stunts are filmed with multicamera setups. These shots are usually very dangerous or costly, and there is only one chance to photograph them. By filming with more than one camera and from many different angles, the director is usually assured that there will be enough coverage of the scene for editing purposes.

Many of the television situation comedies (sitcoms) that are filmed in front of a live audience use multiple cameras.

Mutar   A 16mm lens attachment that is designed for use on a Zeiss 10mm-to-100mm zoom lens. It is used to increase the angle of view of the lens and to make it more wide-angle than it already is. The lens is placed in its macro setting before the mutar is attached. Focus is then adjusted by turning the zoom barrel of the lens instead of the focus barrel.

NABET   See *National Alliance of Broadcast Employees and Technicians.*

National Alliance of Broadcast Employees and Technicians (NABET)   A national labor organization which was originally created for radio technicians. It was later expanded to include television and feature film technicians. Most of the larger television and feature film productions are still governed by IATSE, but there are some productions which come under NABET rules and regulations.

ND   See *neutral density filter.*

negative   Film that, when processed, produces a negative image of the scene. A print must be made of this negative for viewing purposes. This term is sometimes used to refer to unexposed raw stock used for most film productions.

neutral density filter (ND)   A filter used to reduce the amount of light that strikes the film. It has no effect on colors. Neutral density filters are gray in color and come in varying densities. Neutral density filters require an exposure compensation depending on the number and the density of the filter; ND 3 requires one stop, ND 6, two stops, and ND 9, three stops.

9.5mm   The gauge of an early film that was used for amateur cinematography. It was introduced in 1922 in France and was very popular in Europe. It was eventually replaced by 8 mm film stock.

NG   See *no good.*

niner light   See *lens light.*

nitrate-base film   A highly flammable film stock used in the early days of filmmaking. It was made of cellulose nitrate, which was capable of self-igniting under certain circumstances. It is no longer used for the manufacture of motion picture film. The newer film stocks are composed of a triacetate base.

no good (NG)   Any take that is not printed or not circled on the camera report. There may have been a technical problem during shooting, or possibly the performance was not acceptable to the director. On the daily film-inventory report form, NG refers to the total amount of footage for all takes on the camera report that are not to be printed or transferred by the lab.

nonunion   Any film production that has not signed an agreement with either of the technical unions (IATSE or NABET) for the crew or with the Screen Actors Guild (SAG) for the cast. Many union members still work on nonunion productions, but they do not have the union to back them up if there are any problems during filming. Most nonunion productions pay a lower wage and work longer hours per day than union-regulated productions.

obie light   A light that is mounted directly on the camera right over the matte box (Figure O.1). It is used to give a highlight to the actor's eyes. See also *eyelight*.

O'Connor   The trade name for a brand of fluid camera heads and tripods used in professional film production (Figures F.2, B.1).

on call   Term used for any members of the cast or crew who may or may not be needed for work on a certain day, but still must be available in case they are called. Many times, an on call person is paid the normal salary so that he or she will be available if needed.

Figure O.1   Panavision Panalite (obie light). (Courtesy of Panavision, Inc.)

1.85 (one-eight-five)   The standard aspect ratio for today's theatrical motion pictures. It may also be written as 1.85:1, which means that the picture area is 1.85 times as wide as it is high (Figure A.1). When filming in 1.85 format, standard spherical lenses and equipment may be used.

one-inch lens (1-inch lens)   A slang term used in the early days of filmmaking to indicate a 25mm lens. The term is still used today by some cameramen.

one-light print   A print made from the developed negative with the printer lights set to a single-light setting. This print is usually called the *work print* and is used when doing the rough-cut editing of the film.

opening up the lens   Turning the diaphragm adjustment ring on the lens to a smaller f-stop number, which results in a larger diaphragm opening and allows more light to strike the film.

operator   See *camera operator.*

optical flat   A clear piece of optically corrected glass that is placed in front of the lens to protect the lens. During many types of filming, there may be some kind of object or substance that is projected toward the lens. In order to protect the front of the lens, the optical flat would be placed in the matte box. Because of the special coating on the front of most lenses, it is much easier and less expensive to replace the optical flat than to replace a lens. The optical flat may also be put in front of the lens to help reduce the sound coming from the camera; since most of the sound comes out from the lens port opening. This makes the sound mixer's job a little easier. The optical flat is available in the same sizes as most filters and should be included in the filter order on any film production.

orangewood sticks   Wooden sticks that are used to remove emulsion build-up in the gate or aperture plate. The gate or aperture plate should only be cleaned with these sticks and never with any type of metal or sharp instrument.

orthochromatic   Early black-and-white film that is more sensitive to some colors than to others. A bright blue or green object may appear white on orthochromatic film. The less green or blue in an object would make it appear more black on film.

out of sync   A term used to indicate that the picture and sound track are not synchronized. Being out of sync is especially noticeable when an actor on screen is speaking because the movement of the actor's mouth does not match the words on the sound track.

overcrank   Running the camera at a speed that is higher than normal sync speed. This causes the action to appear in slow motion when it is projected at sync speed of 24 fps. The term originated in the early days of filmmaking when all cameras were cranked by hand.

overexpose   Allowing too much light to strike the film as it is being exposed. This results in the photographic image having a washed-out look or being much lighter than normal. The director of photography may overexpose the film in order to achieve a desired effect. It is much better to overexpose the film stock than to underexpose it because, with overexposed film, there is more latitude to correct any problems when printing or transferring the final film.

over-the-shoulder shot   A shot filmed from behind one of the actors, so that you see part of the actor's head and shoulder in the frame. During filming, any scene that has two or more actors speaking with each other usually will involve shooting over-the-shoulder shots for each actor in the scene.

PA See *production assistant.*

pan The horizontal, or left-and-right, movement of the camera. The camera is usually mounted to either a geared head or fluid head, which is on the tripod or dolly. The geared head contains a wheel that is turned to move the camera either left or right. The fluid head contains a handle that enables the operator to make the pan moves, by moving the handle either left or right. By panning the camera during the shot, the camera operator is able to follow the action within the scene.

Panafinder Trade name of a director's viewfinder manufactured by Panavision. It is the kind of viewfinder that allows the lens to be placed on it for viewing and lining up the shot. See also *director's viewfinder.*

Panaglow Trade name used by Panavision for the illuminated frame lines of the ground glass. When filming in low-light situations, Panaglow can be turned on so it is easier for the camera operator to frame the shot.

Panalite Trade name for the camera-mounted light manufactured by Panavision (Figure O.1). See also *Obie light.*

Panatate Trade name of a specialized piece of motion picture camera equipment manufactured by Panavision. It is a special type of camera mount that allows the camera to rotate 360 degrees around the axis of the lens (Figures P.1, P.2). The camera may also be panned and tilted in the normal manner.

Panavision Manufacturer and distributor of motion picture cameras and specialized equipment. The Panavision *Platinum* camera is one of the quietest cameras in the film industry. Panavision equipment is most often used by the major studios and larger production companies on large-budget films and television series. Panavision will assist smaller production companies who are interested in using Panavision equipment but who do not have the big budgets of the larger companies or studios. Some of the most commonly used Panavision cameras

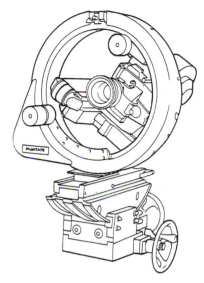

Figure P.1 Front view of Panavision Panatate rotating camera mount. (Courtesy of Panavision, Inc.)

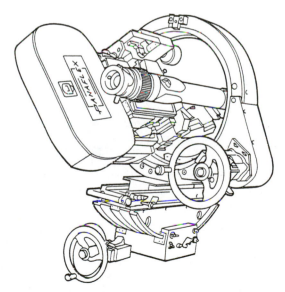

Figure P.2 Rear view of Panavision Panatate rotating camera mount. (Courtesy of Panavision, Inc.)

Figure P.3   Panavision Panastar 35mm high-speed camera. (Courtesy of Panavision, Inc.)

Figure P.4   Panavision Platinum 35mm camera. (Courtesy of Panavision, Inc.)

Figure P.5   Panavision System 65 camera. (Courtesy of Panavision, Inc.)

are the *Panaflex-16* for 16mm and the *Platinum, Golden, Panastar* and *Panflex-X* for 35mm (Figures P.3-P.5).

pancake   See *apple box*.

panchromatic   Current black-and-white films that respond equally to all colors. It reproduces each color of the scene in its equivalent shade of gray.

Panther   Trade name for a brand of camera dolly manufactured by Panther Corporation (Figure D.11).

paper tape, quarter-inch   Tape that is most often used to make focus marks on the lens. It is wrapped around the barrel of the lens so that it can be marked for following focus.

paper tape, half-inch or one-inch   Tape that can be used for making actor's marks, for labeling equipment, or for any other taping job during production.

paper tape, two-inch   Tape that is used for the same types of things as gaffer tape. It can be used for hanging items on painted walls because the glue is not as strong as that on gaffer tape, and so it will not remove paint when taken down. It may also be used to seal any cracks or holes in the darkroom. See also *gaffer tape*.

parallax   The difference or displacement between what the operator sees through the viewfinder and what the camera sees through the lens. Parallax is more apparent on close-up shots than on wide-angle shots. This phenomenon occurs when a separate viewfinder on the side of the camera is used instead of a through-the-lens viewfinder.

per diem   Money paid to actors and crew members when they are working on a distant location. This money is used for basic living expenses, such as meals and laundry. Per diem is paid in addition to the salary of the actor or crew member and is paid for each day the crew is on location, whether it is a work day or not.

perforations (perfs)   Also called **sprocket holes**. Equally spaced holes that are cut into the edges of the film along the entire length of the roll (Figure P.6). These holes are engaged by the teeth of the sprockets, in the film magazines and camera movements, allowing the film to accurately travel through the camera before and after exposure. In 35mm film, there are four perforations per film frame, on each edge, and in 16mm, there are two per frame on each edge.

persistence of vision   The phenomenon that allows the human eye to retain an image for a brief moment after it has been viewed. This allows

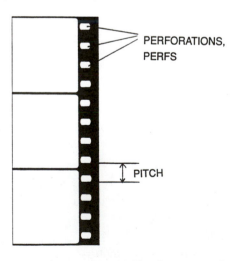

Figure P.6   Enlarged view of 35mm film showing perforations and pitch. (Not drawn to scale.) (Courtesy of Panavision, Inc.)

the illusion of movement when a series of still pictures are projected on a screen at a specified rate of speed. At normal sync speed of 24 fps, a series of still frames projected on a screen appear, to the human eye, to be moving continuously.

photo double   See *double.*

pick-up shot   Any shot that is filmed after the completion of the principal photography on a film. Pick-up shots may be insert shots that do not require any actors. They also may be shots needed to fix any gaps or holes in the film that were discovered during the editing process.

picture car   Any motor vehicle, car, truck, and so on, that is going to be filmed during production. They are not the same as the vehicles used behind the scenes to transport people and equipment.

pilot   Usually the first episode of a television series, which is shown to get the viewer interested in the show. Many TV pilots are filmed as a two-hour movie to introduce the main characters and story line to the television audience.

pitch   The distance between the bottom edge of one perforation and the bottom edge of the next perforation (Figure P.6). This distance is measured along the length of the film.

point of view (POV)   A shot filmed at a specific camera angle so that the action or object appears to be seen from the actor's viewpoint. A point-of-view shot usually means a shot that is seen out of someone's eyes.

polarizing filter   A filter that is used to reduce glare and reflections from shiny surfaces. It may be used when filming into or through a window. It is also used to enhance or darken a blue sky or water. It is mounted so that it can be rotated until the desired effect is achieved. While looking through the lens, the director of photography or camera operator rotates the filter until the correct or desired effect is achieved. An exposure compensation of one and two-thirds to two stops is required.

positive   A print made from a film negative; may also refer to a film that is shot by using reversal film in the camera.

post-production   The period after principal photography has been completed on a film. During this time, all editing, looping, scoring, mixing, and so on, are completed in order to finish the film.

POV   See *point of view.*

powder puffs   Soft make-up type-pads that are used to erase information that has been written on an acrylic slate with erasable slate markers. The puffs are usually attached to the slate marker to make it easier for use.

practical   A term usually used to refer to a set or location light that is actually working in the scene. It may be a lamp on a table or a ceiling light in a room.

precision speed control   A speed-control attachment that allows the speed of the camera to be varied to a precise degree, sometimes to three decimal places. It may be used when filming high-speed or slow motion. It can also be used when filming a television screen or computer monitor in order to synchronize the camera with the video image.

pre-production   The period of time before actual filming begins. Pre-production involves preparing a budget, choosing equipment, casting the actors, hiring the crew, scouting locations, constructing sets, and anything else that needs to be done so that principal photography may start on time.

prep   Also called **camera prep**. The time during pre-production when the equipment is checked to be sure that it is in working order. During the camera prep, the first camera assistant goes to the camera rental house and sets up and tests all of the camera equipment to be sure that it is in proper working order for filming.

pressure plate   A flat, smoothly polished piece of metal that puts pressure on the film keeping it flat against the aperture plate and steady as it travels through the gate. It is usually spring loaded and is located behind the aperture plate inside the camera. Many times the pressure plate is a part of the film magazine. Without this plate keeping the film flat and steady as it travels through the camera, the photographic image would be unsteady or blurred and out of focus.

primary colors   For the purposes of cinematography, red, blue, and green. When these three colors of light are combined, they form what is known as white light. The corresponding complementary colors to these are cyan, yellow, and magenta, respectively. See also *complementary colors.*

prime lens   A lens of a single, fixed focal length. Examples of prime lenses are 25mm, 35mm, 50mm, 75mm, 100mm, and so on.

principal photography   The period of production when all filming of the scripted action takes place.

print   A positive copy made from a film negative. When the film is sent to the lab for developing, a negative copy results. For viewing purposes, a positive print must be made of the film.

print all   The instructions that tell the lab to print all of the takes on a given roll of exposed film.

print circle takes only   The instructions that tell the lab to print only the takes that have been circled on the camera report, for a specific roll of film.

"Print it"   What the director calls out after a shot to indicate that he is pleased with the performance and wants the take printed by the lab. When this command is given, the script supervisor makes a note on the script, and the second camera assistant circles the take number and the footage amount on the camera report.

printer lights   The controls on the laboratory printer that are adjusted during the processing of the film to correct for any differences in the density of the negative.

production   The period of time during which all aspects of a feature film or television show are done. This includes all aspects of pre-production and post-production and also the actual filming or shooting period of the production. Production may also refer to the name of the film or show that is being worked on.

production assistant (PA)   Also called **gopher**; **runner**. An entry-level crew position that involves doing the many small but necessary jobs for the producer or production manager. This includes making copies, picking up supplies, delivering scripts to the actors, and running any errands that are necessary to the production.

production company   A company that is responsible for all aspects of producing a film or television show. The company may be one of the big studios or production companies, or it may be a smaller independent company.

production number   The number of the film or television episode as assigned by the production company. If a production company has more than one project being filmed at one time, each project will be assigned a different number so that the company can keep track of the various expenses and things needed for each project. When filming a weekly television series, each weekly episode is given a new production number.

production title   The working title of a film as assigned by the production company.

Professional Camerman's Handbook   An indispensable manual used by both camera assistants and directors of photography. It contains illustrations and descriptions of the many different cameras and related pieces of equipment in use today. For each camera, it describes how to load the magazine with film and how to thread it in the camera.

Pro Mist filter   A diffusion filter that is used to soften harsh lines in an actor's face. It may sometimes give the illusion of the image being out of focus. Pro Mist filters come in varying densities and are available in white and black diffusion. No exposure compensation is required.

pull   During the developing of the film, the act of decreasing the development time, or under-developing it, by allowing it to remain in the developer for a shorter period of time. It is the same as treating the film as if it had a lower ASA rating. Pulling the film is a procedure that alters the exposure on the original negative and is usually done in increments of one stop.

pulldown claws   The small hooks or pins, located in the camera movement, that reach into the perforations of the film and pull the film down into position in the gate so that it may be photographed. When the film is in place in the gate, the pulldown claws retract and the registration pins hold the film in the gate for exposure. Once the film has been exposed, the registration pins retract and the pulldown claw pulls the next frame into position (Figures P.7, P.8).

pulling focus   See *follow focus.*

push   During the developing of the film, the act of increasing the development time, or over-developing it, by allowing it to remain in the

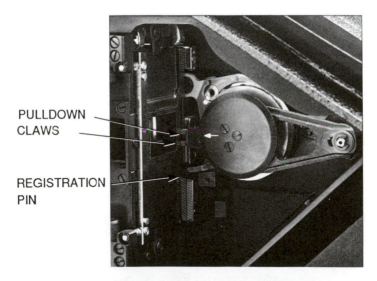

PULLDOWN CLAWS

REGISTRATION PIN

Figure P.7   Arriflex 35-3 movement showing pulldown claws and registration pin. (Photo courtesy of the Arriflex Corporation.)

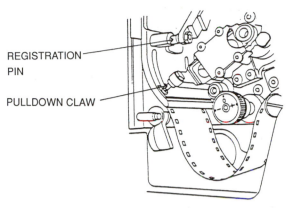

REGISTRATION
PIN

PULLDOWN CLAW

Figure P.8 Panavision 35mm movement showing pulldown claw and registration pin. (Courtesy of Panavision, Inc.)

developer for a longer period of time. It is the same as treating the film as if it had a higher ASA rating. The result gives a grainier image, but sometimes this is the only way to get the image on film. Pushing the film is a procedure that alters the exposure on the original negative and is usually done in increments of one stop.

"Quiet on the set" What the first assistant director calls out to let the cast and crew know that it is time to stop talking and prepare for filming the shot. While the crew is working to prepare everything for shooting, the noise level on the set may become very high. Calling for quiet helps to keep the noise level down between takes and lets the director and cast concentrate better. Once filming has begun, no crew member should talk or make a sound, otherwise it will be picked up by the sound recorder microphones.

rack focus   It involves turning the barrel of the lens so that an object in the frame comes into focus. Many times in a film you may see a shot where an actor in the foreground turns to look at something behind him. At the moment he turns, you see the focus shift from his face to the object in the background. This change in focus is known as a rack focus. See also *follow focus*.

rackover viewing system   The viewing system, used in older cameras, that allowed the entire camera body to move independent of the lens so that the camera operator could view the shot during rehearsals. This allowed the operator to line up the shot exactly as it would be filmed but did not allow viewing through the lens during filming. Once the shot was lined up, the camera and lens were re-aligned so that the lens was positioned in front of the film. This system is used today only for special-effects filming. The newer film cameras all have reflex, or through-the-lens, viewing systems. See also *viewfinder*.

raincover   A waterproof cover used to protect the camera in extreme weather conditions, including snow and rain. It has an opening for the viewfinder eyepiece and contains clear panels for the assistant to view the lens markings. The front of the cover is open so that the lens is not obstructed.

rain deflector   A special device that is placed in front of the lens and is used to keep water from hitting the lens when filming in the rain. It uses a high-speed rotating glass disk that flings the water off as fast as it hits and so keeps the lens clear of the water.

raw stock   Fresh, unexposed and unprocessed film stock.

reaction shot   Usually, a close-up shot of an actor who is reacting to something off camera or in another shot. It is used to show an actor's response to some action within the scene.

reflected light Any light that is bouncing off, or being reflected by, an object. Reflected light is usually measured with a reflected light meter called a spot meter. See also *spot meter.*

reflex camera Any camera that allows viewing through the lens during filming. The camera contains a mirrored shutter, which directs the image to the viewfinder for the camera operator to see the shot.

reflex viewing system A viewing system that allows the camera operator to view the image as it is being filmed. The image is reflected to the viewfinder, usually by a mirror shutter, allowing the camera operator to see the image through the lens. Because the image is sent to the viewfinder intermittently, there is a slight flicker in the viewfinder while the camera is running. The advantage to this type of viewing system is that the operator can see the image exactly as it is being recorded on the film. It eliminates the problems associated with the older rackover viewing system. See also *viewfinder.*

registration The accurate positioning of the film in the film gate as it is running through the camera. Any variation will cause a jump or blur in the photographic image. During the camera prep, the registration may be checked by filming a registration chart and then viewing the results.

registration chart A chart containing a series of crossed lines that is used during the camera prep to check the registration of the camera (Figure R.1). A double-exposed image of the chart will show if the registration of the camera is accurate.

registration pin Part of the camera movement, consisting of a small metal spike or pin, that holds the film securely in the gate while it is being

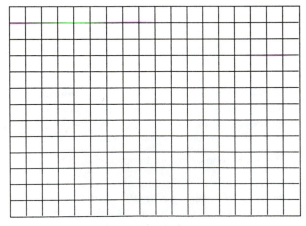

Figure R.1   Example of registration chart.

exposed. Most cameras contain a single registration pin, while some of the cameras used for special-effects cinematography contain two registration pins. These special cameras are referred to as dual-pin-registered cameras. While the pulldown claw is bringing the film down into the gate, the registration pin retracts to allow the film to move. When the new frame of film is positioned in the gate, the pulldown claw retracts and the registration pin engages the perforation to hold the film for the time it is being exposed (Figures P.7, P.8). See also *pulldown claw.*

rehearsal A period of time prior to filming when the dialogue and actions within a scene are practiced. This is done many times until the director is satisfied with the performance. Dialogue rehearsals may be done many weeks before actual filming and then again on the set just before shooting the scene. When rehearsing on the set, the crew stands back and watches so that they know what will be involved when the scene is filmed. The DP determines the lighting based on the actor's positions in the scene. The 1st AC measures the distance from the camera for each actor's position so that he may follow focus during the shot. The 2nd AC places tape marks for each actor's position.

release print The final print of a film, complete with picture, sound, and all effects, that is distributed to theaters for showing to the public.

remote switch A camera switch, usually connected to a long cable running from the camera, that allows starting and stopping the camera from a distance (Figure R.2). They can be used when the camera operator cannot be right next to the camera during the shot, for example, when filming dangerous shots or when filming car shots.

reveal A shot that is done to show something important in the frame, something that was not previously visible. It may involve panning or

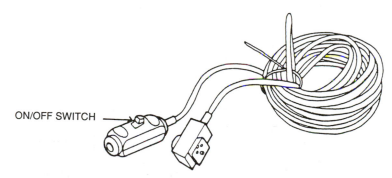

ON/OFF SWITCH

Figure R.2 Remote on/off switch. (Courtesy of Panavision, Inc.)

tilting the camera, dollying or zooming to show the action or object being revealed.

reversal   Also called **positive**; **positive film**. Film that, when processed, produces a positive image of the scene. It may be viewed directly.

reverse angle   A shot that is photographed from an angle opposite to that of the angle of the previous shot. It is most often used for dialogue scenes between two actors, so that the editor may cut from one actor speaking to the other one speaking.

right-hand grip   A camera accessory item used when filming hand-held shots. As the name implies, it attaches to the right-hand side of the camera and is used to hold the camera steady during shooting. Most right-hand grips contain an on/off switch for the camera operator to start and stop the camera (Figure R.3).

rocker plate   A low-angle camera mount that usually consists of two separate pieces: a top section, which has a curved base allowing it to rock back and forth; and a bottom cradle, which swivels left and right and into which the top section fits (Figure R.4). The combined movement of rocking the camera back and forth and swiveling the base left and right allows the camera operator to make smooth pans and tilts from very low angles without using a fluid head or geared head.

"Roll" ("Roll camera," "Rolling," "Roll please")   What the 1st AD calls out to indicate that filming is about to start for a shot. The standard procedure when this is called is for the sound mixer to start the recorder and call out "Speed" when it has reached sound speed. At this point, the camera operator will start the camera and call out "Rolling" when

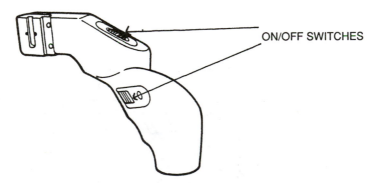

ON/OFF SWITCHES

Figure R.3   Right-hand grip for hand-held camera. (Courtesy of Panavision, Inc.)

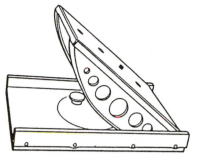

Figure R.4   Rocker plate. (Courtesy of Panavision, Inc.)

it has reached sync speed. The 2nd AC will call out "Marker" and then clap the slate. The director will then call out "Action" as an indication to the actors to begin the scene.

roll number   The number assigned to a roll of film when it is placed on the camera. Each time a new roll of film is placed on the camera, the next higher number is assigned to that roll. On the first day of shooting, the first roll placed on the camera is roll number 1, the next is number 2, and so on. When using more than one camera, the rolls are numbered by using a combination of the camera letter designation and the roll number for that particular camera; for example, all rolls placed on the A-camera would be labeled A-1, A-2, A-3, and so on, and all rolls placed on the B-camera would be labeled B-1, B-2, B-3, and so on. If a roll of film is removed from the camera for any reason and then later placed back on the camera without breaking the film, the roll number remains the same.

Ronford/Baker   The trade name of a brand of motion picture camera fluid heads and tripods. One of the most commonly used heads is the *Ronford 7.*

room tone   The ambient sound present in a particular room or set. Every room contains its own background noise, which is not usually heard by the average listener. At the completion of filming in a particular room or set, the sound mixer will record a few minutes of this ambient sound to be used during the editing process to help hide any cuts in the sound track and to help the film sound more realistic. See also *ambience.*

rough cut   A very rough version of the edited film that contains all of the scenes in their approximate order. The rough cut may not contain all music or sound effects; it may be used to determine if any additional scenes or shots are needed in order to make the story flow better. The rough cut will probably be edited many times to correct the pacing and timing of the film.

rubber donut   See *donut.*

run-by shot   A shot of a vehicle driving by the camera while the camera is in a stationary position; may also refer to a shot from a moving camera as it passes by a certain point. The camera may be mounted onto a camera car, or it may be in a picture car as it is being driven.

runner   See *production assistant.*

running shot   A traveling shot that has the camera moving to keep up with an actor or object moving in the frame. The camera may be mounted on a dolly or camera car in order to achieve this type of shot.

rushes   See *dailies.*

Sachtler The trade name of a brand of motion picture camera fluid heads and tripods (Figures F.3, F.4).

SAG See *Screen Actors Guild.*

Samuelson MKII Calculator Trade name of a brand of depth-of-field calculator used by most 1st ACs.

scale The minimum wage, as established by the unions, for cast and crew members. When working on a union production, a member of the cast or crew cannot be paid less than scale. On the average, an experienced crew member or well-known actor or actress will be paid much more than scale.

scene A section of the film as it takes place in a particular location or time in the story.

scene number The number assigned to a scene, based on its place in the script. Normally, each time a scene's location or time changes, a new scene number is assigned to the action. When filming a small portion of a scene that has already been shot, the scene number is a combination of the scene number and a letter of the alphabet. The first time a portion of a scene is shot, it is assigned the letter A, then B, and so on. For slating purposes, the scene number is written on the slate and on the camera report as a reference to which scenes have been filmed on which roll of film.

scratches Grooves or lines on a film's surface that can distort the image. Watching a film that contains scratches is very distracting to the viewer. In most instances, any film scratches detected indicate that those shots containing the scratch must be shot again. A film scratch can be caused by many different things, including film chips or metal burrs in the magazine or gate area of the camera. A small imperfection in the aperture plate may cause a fine piece of emulsion to scrape off the film creating a scratch on the film emulsion. It is standard practice to check the gate of the camera and the film on a regular basis to be sure that there are no scratches. Most 1st ACs check the gate after each printed take.

Screen Actors Guild (SAG)   The union that sets the wages, working conditions, benefits, and so on, for all performers working in the motion picture and televison industries.

screening   A private showing of a finished film, usually for the cast and crew and special invited guests, which may include studio executives and distributors.

script supervisor   The member of the film crew who keeps track of the action for each scene. The script supervisor keeps notes for each shot regarding actor movement and the placement of props. Notes are also kept regarding the number of takes for each scene, which takes are to be printed as requested by the director, the camera and sound roll numbers, the lens used, filters used, and so on. By paying close attention to detail during each shot, the script supervisor ensures that continuity is maintained from shot to shot and scene to scene. During actual shooting, the script supervisor tells the 2nd AC what the scene and take number is for each shot. When the director chooses to print certain takes, he will instruct the script supervisor who will then tell the 2nd AC to circle these takes on the camera report.

SE   See *short end.*

2nd AC   See *second camera assistant.*

2nd AD   See *second assistant director.*

second assistant director (2nd AD)   The assistant to the 1st AD. The 2nd AD usually prepares and distributes the various paperwork involved in the production. This includes call sheets, production reports, actor's sign-in sheets, and so on. The 2nd AD assists the 1st AD in positioning extras for a scene and also in guiding the extras through any movements that they must make during the scene.

second camera   An additional camera used for filming shots or scenes at the same time as the primary, or main, camera. Most productions are filmed using only one camera, which is moved for each new shot or setup. By using a second camera, two different shots can be filmed at the same time; for example, one camera may be shooting a master shot while the second camera is shooting a closeup of one of the actors. The second camera may also be used when filming shots or scenes that can only be staged once (car stunts, fire shots, explosions, etc.).

second camera assistant (second assistant camerman) (2nd AC)   The member of the camera crew whose duties include assisting the 1st AC, clapping the slate for the shot, keeping camera reports, placing marks for actors, and loading and unloading film into the magazines. The 2nd AC reports directly to the 1st AC during production.

"Second marker" What the 2nd AC calls out when slating a shot if the first slate was missed by the camera operator or sound mixer. Sometimes the camera operator may not frame the slate properly, that is, so it is completely visible in the frame. There may be times that the 2nd AC claps the sticks before either sound or camera are rolling. In any of these cases, the sticks must be clapped a second time, and this term is called out as an indication to the editor that the slate was clapped twice.

second second An additional 2nd AC hired for the production. Many times, when any additional cameras are used, a second second is hired to assist the original 2nd AC in carrying out the duties of that position. In many cases, one of the second assistants will remain on the set at all times while the other is responsible for all of the loading and unloading of film magazines. See also *second camera assistant.*

second unit A separate production crew hired to film sequences that do not require the presence of the director or principal actors. This may include filming insert shots, large-scale action sequences, establishing shots of various locations, and so on. In most cases, a second-unit director is hired to direct these sequences.

Sekonic Trade name of a brand of exposure meters.

set light Any light that is used to illuminate the background or any area of the set. The set light or lights help to add some depth to the shot and also give a natural look to the surroundings.

shooting company The production crew of a motion picture or television series.

shooting ratio The ratio of the total amount of film shot on a production to the total amount used in the completed, edited film. Suppose that 100,000 feet of film, or more, are used to shoot a feature film that will be 2 hours long in its completed form and contain 10,800 feet of film. This is a shooting ratio of 100,000:10,800, or approximately 10:1. Usually, a 4:1 or 5:1 shooting ratio is considered economical.

shoulder pad A small pad that attaches to the underside of the camera for use during hand-held shots. It is used to make the camera operator more comfortable when the camera is on his or her shoulder for long periods of time. If a shoulder pad is not available, a rolled-up jacket or towel or any other padding can be used.

short end (SE) A roll of unexposed raw stock that is less than a full-size roll but larger than a waste roll or dummy load. In 16mm, a short end is usually any roll larger than 40 feet, and in 35mm, it is usually any roll larger than 100 feet.

short eyepiece   A smaller version of the camera eyepiece that is used especially when filming hand-held shots. It may also be used on the camera in certain filming situations where the long eyepiece is too uncomfortable or in an awkward position (Figure E.4).

shutter   The mechanical device in a camera that rotates during filming to alternately block light from the film and then allow light to strike the film. Many shutters contain a mirror that reflects some of the light so that it enters the eyepiece, allowing the camera operator to view the shot during filming. As the shutter turns, it alternately blocks the light from the eyepiece, allowing it to strike the film, and then blocks the light from the film, allowing it to go to the eyepiece. This causes a slight flicker in the eyepiece when viewing the shot during filming.

shutter angle   A measurement in degrees of the open part of the camera shutter (Figure S.1). For most professional cinematography, the standard shutter angle is 180°. Many cameras contain fixed shutters that cannot be changed or adjusted. Some cameras have an adjustable shutter angle to allow for special types of filming. Some of the cameras that have adjustable shutters include the *Panavision Platinum, Panavision Golden,* and the *Arriflex 535.*

shutter speed   The exposure time of the shutter while the camera runs at a specific speed. The standard shutter speed, or exposure time, for motion pictures is 1/50th of a second at sync speed of 24 fps.

silicone   A type of lubricant that is available in a spray or liquid form. The spray is used to lubricate the sliding base plate or tripod legs if they begin to stick and should never be used on any of the moving parts of

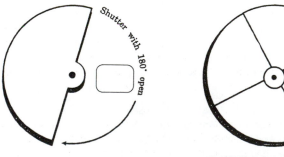

Standard, 180° fixed shutter   Double-bladed, variable shutter

Figure S.1   Examples of shutter angle.

the camera motor or movement. The liquid type is usually used to lubricate the pulldown claws of some cameras, including *Panavision* and *Ultracam*. When using silicone on the camera pulldown claw, only the type recommended for the particular camera should be used.

single   Coverage of a scene that usually involves shooting a closeup of each individual actor in the scene. It may be a shot of the actor delivering lines or reacting to another actor in the scene. A single can also be a medium shot or any other type of shot as long as there is only one person in the shot.

16mm   A film gauge, introduced in 1923, that is used mainly for nontheatrical productions. It is most commonly used for music videos and commercials, and, today, many television series are shooting with 16mm film. Because of the lower price of the film stock as well as the lower price of renting the camera equipment, 16mm film provides a less expensive filming alternative to 35mm film. For television broadcast or video-cassette release, it can provide very good results. It contains 40 frames per foot, and each frame has two perforations on each side of the film. At normal sync speed of 24 fps, 16mm film will travel through the camera at the rate of 36 feet per minute.

65mm/70mm   A film gauge that is most often used for release prints of theatrical films. It is very rarely used for actual productions. There are some 65mm cameras available for filming for any production company that would like to shoot with 65mm. Panavision is one company that still has 65mm cameras available for filming (Figure P.5).

slate   A board marked with the pertinent identifying information for each scene photographed. It should contain the film's title, director's name, cameraman's name, date, camera roll number, scene number, and take number. The two main types of slates are sync and insert. The sync slate usually contains two hinged pieces of wood that are clapped together at the beginning of all sound or sync shots (Figure S.10). These two pieces of wood are usually called the clapsticks. During filming, the slate is held in front of the camera, at the beginning of each shot. When the sound recorder and camera are running at sync speed, the 2nd AC calls out "Marker" and claps the wooden sticks together. Once the slate has been clapped together, the director then calls "Action" as an indication to the actors to begin the scene. The insert slate is a smaller version of the sync slate and it usually does not contain the clapsticks (Figure I.3). See also *insert slate; sync slate.*

slate markers   Erasable markers that are used to mark information on acrylic slates. It is usually some type of dry-erase marker. The two most common brands of slate markers are *Expo* and *Rite On/Wipe Off* markers.

sliding base plate   An attachment used for mounting the camera to the head (Figure S.2, S.3). It is usually a two-part plate with the bottom piece mounted to the tripod head and the top piece mounted to the camera. It allows sliding the camera forward or backward on the head to properly balance the camera with its different-sized lenses and magazines. By achieving proper balance, the camera operator does not have to struggle in order to make smooth pan and tilt moves.

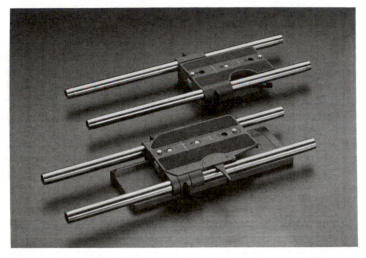

Figure S.2   Arriflex sliding base plates. (Photo courtesy of the Arriflex Corporation.)

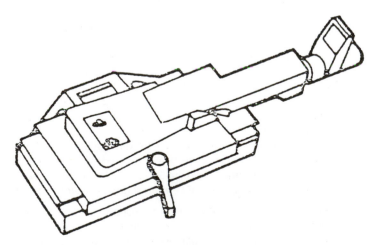

Figure S.3   Panavision sliding balance plate. (Courtesy of Panavision, Inc.

slow motion   An effect that gives the illusion that the action is moving at a much slower speed than what is considered normal. It is achieved by running the film through the camera at a speed faster than the normal sync speed of 24 fps. When this film is then projected at normal speed, it appears to be moving much slower. It is used many times in sporting events to demonstrate the skill of an athlete or to review a key moment of a ball game. For movies and television, it is most often used for an artistic effect or when filming any action sequences or stunts to make them appear to be lasting longer on screen.

SMPTE   See *Society of Motion Picture and Television Engineers.*

Society of Motion Picture and Television Engineers   A professional organization that sets and defines the technical standards for the television and motion picture industry.

soft focus   Indicates a shot or scene that appears to be out of focus to the viewer's eye. It is usually caused by the 1st AC or the focus puller not setting the lens focus properly so that the image is fuzzy and lacks any sharp detail around the edges. It is not the same as a shot that is made with some type of a diffusion filter in front of the lens in order to create a specific soft or dreamlike effect. If a soft-focus shot is noticed during shooting, it is usually standard practice to check the focus by eye and also to measure the distance and then do the shot over again correctly. A soft-focus shot that is not noticed until the next day's screening of dailies may create many problems for the production company, including rescheduling actors and locations, transportation of cast and crew, rebuilding sets, and so on, in order to shoot the scene or shot over again.

"Sound speed"   What the sound mixer calls out when the sound recorder has reached the proper sync speed required for filming. When the 1st AD calls for quiet on the set and for the camera to roll, the sound mixer turns on the recorder and calls "Sound speed" at the appropriate time. When the camera operator hears this, he then turns on the camera, the shot is slated, and "Action" is then called by the director. See also *"Speed."*

sound stage   An enclosed, soundproof building that is used for the production of motion pictures and television. Most major film studios contain many sound stages of various sizes for filming purposes. In most cases, the sound stage is used for filming interior scenes, but they may also be used for exterior scenes.

space blanket   A large cover used to protect the camera and equipment from the sun and weather. It is usually a bright silver color on one side and may be red, green, blue, or another color on the opposite side. In bright sunlight, the cover is used with the silver side facing towards the sun to reflect the sun and help to keep the camera cool. When placing the cover on the camera with the silver side toward the camera, the heat from the sun is absorbed, which keeps the camera warm in cooler situations.

Spectra　Trade name of a brand of exposure meter (Figures I.2, S.6).

"Speed"　What the camera operator calls out after the camera has been turned on and has reached the proper sync speed. It may also be used by the sound mixer to indicate that the sound recorder has reached sync speed. See also *Sound speed.*

speed (camera)　The rate at which the film travels through the camera. Standard film speed in the United States is 24 fps. For 16mm film, this translates to 36 feet per minute, and for 35mm film, it is 90 feet per minute.

speed (film)　An indication of the film's sensitivity to light. The film speed may be referred to as the ASA, DIN, or EI number. The higher the number, the faster is the film's speed and the more sensitive it is to light.

speed (lens)　The f-stop or t-stop number of the lens setting at its widest opening. The smaller this number, the faster the lens is. Fast lenses are used many times for filming in extreme low-light situations.

speed crank　Also called **L-handle**. An "L" shaped handle that attaches to the follow-focus mechanism (Figure S.4). It is used when the 1st AC or

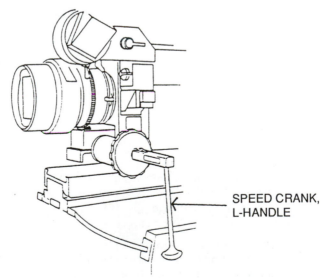

SPEED CRANK,
L-HANDLE

Figure S.4　Speed crank or L-handle. (Courtesy of Panavision, Inc.)

focus puller has a very long focus change to do during a shot. It is much easier for the 1st AC to perform a long focus shift by turning the handle of the crank, than by repeatedly turning the knob of the follow-focus mechanism.

spider   See *spreader.*

split diopter   A type of filter that may be used to maintain focus on two objects, one in the foreground and one in the background. It is used the same way that a regular diopter is used in that it will allow the lens to focus on a foreground object that is much closer than would normally be possible. The split diopter is round in shape, and only half of it contains the diopter. The remaining half of the filter is clear. The diopter side allows focusing on the foreground object while the clear side allows focusing on the background object. As with diopters, the split diopters are available in varying strengths—the higher the number, the closer the lens can be to the object in focus. Some experimentation is required in order to determine which diopter will work for a specific shooting situation. No exposure compensation is required. See also *split focus.*

split focus   The technique of setting the focus so that a foreground object and a background object are both in focus for a shot or scene. It is used in place of a split diopter or when the split diopter may not work for the particular situation. By setting the focus to a point in between the two objects, you may be able to keep them both in focus. Split focus is not possible in every shooting situation. It will depend on the distance between the subjects, the lens used, the f-stop setting on the lens, and the depth of field for the particular situation. The DP usually decides if a split focus should be tried for a shot. See also *split diopter.*

spot meter   An exposure meter that takes a light reading by measuring the light that is reflected by an object. It is called a spot meter because it takes its measurement from a very small area of the object (Figures S.5, S.6). This small area is called the angle of acceptance, and, in most cases, it is around 1°. When using a spot meter, it is usual to stand at the position of the camera and point the meter toward the object. See also *exposure meter; light meter.*

spreader   Also called **spider; triangle**. A metal or rubber device that has three arms and opens up to form a horizontal Y-shape to support the legs of the tripod (Figure S.7). It prevents the legs of the tripod from slipping out from under the camera. In place of a spreader, many camera assistants use a piece of carpet approximately 4 feet by 4 feet.

sprocket holes   See *perforations.*

Figure S.5 Minolta Spotmeter F spot meter. (Courtesy of Minolta Corporation.)

Figure S.6 Spectra CineSpot spot meter. (Courtesy of Spectra Cine, Inc.)

Figure S.7   Tripod spreader. (Courtesy of Sachtler Corporation.)

sprockets   Small teeth or gears inside the camera or projector that advance the film. The wheels that contain the sprockets, turn and engage with the perforations of the film, moving it through the camera.

Stabilo grease pencil   The brand name of a grease pencil used by many 1st ACs. It is used to make focus marks on lenses or on the white focus-marking disk of the follow focus mechanism. They are available in red, black, white, and yellow.

stand-in   A person who takes the place of a principal actor during the process of placing the camera and lights and setting up the shot. During rehearsals, the stand-in will watch the actor's movements for the scene and then will duplicate them so that the DP may set lights and the camera operator may practice the camera moves. Stand-ins are chosen for their physical similarities to the actor or actress for whom they are standing in. They most often are the same height and weight, have the same hair color, and may also have similar facial features. Many times, the stand-in might be used to double for the actor in long shots or crowd scenes.

standard legs (standard tripod, standards)   The slang term used to indicate the tripod on which the camera and head are mounted (Figures B.1, F.4). They are called standard legs because the tripod is the standard support used when the camera is not mounted on a dolly. Most standard tripods can be adjusted in height from approximately 3 feet to 5 1/2 feet. See also *tripod.*

star filter   A filter placed in front of the lens to give highlights to any lights that appear in the scene. The star filter produces lines coming from bright lights in the scene; the lines depend on the texture of the star filter. A four-point star filter will produce a series of four lines coming from a light source; six-point will produce six lines; and so on. Star filters have a tendency to soften the shot in a way similar to a diffusion filter. No exposure compensation is required for any star filter.

steadicam   A specialized camera-mounting system that includes a special type of harness that allows the camera operator to wear the camera on his body (Figures S.8, S.9). It contains a number of springs and weights that counterbalance the camera and allow the camera operator to do special hand-held-type shots that would not be possible in standard hand-held configuration. Because of the counterbalancing of the camera, the vibration associated with many hand-held shots is eliminated. Some of the shots done with steadicam include running alongside an actor (both forward and backward), following an actor up or down a flight of stairs or a steep hill, following an actor through a crowd of people or down a long winding passageway, and so on. Most steadicam operators must take special classes to learn to use the system. It takes a great deal of practice to become a good steadicam operator. On most films, whenever steadicam is used, a separate operator and assistant are hired for the steadicam shots.

stick-on letters   Plastic or vinyl adhesive-backed letters and numbers that are used to label the slate with production title, director's name, cameraman's name, and date. They are available in many colors,

Figure S.8   Steadicam with Arriflex 35BL camera. (Reprinted from *The ARRI 35 Book*, with permission of the Arriflex Corporation.)

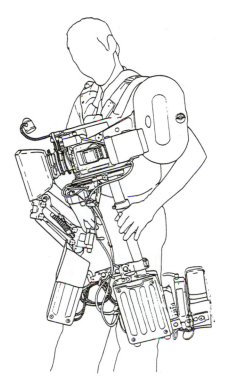

Figure S.9 Steadicam with Arriflex 35-3 camera. (Reprinted from *The ARRI 35 Book*, with permission of the Arriflex Corporation.)

including red, blue, green, black, white, and yellow, and may be 1/2 inch or 3/4 inch high.

stop A shortened form of f-stop or t-stop. See also *f-stop; t-stop.*

stopping down the lens See *closing down the lens.*

stop pull The technique of changing the f-stop or t-stop setting of the lens during a shot. The actor may be moving from a brightly lit area to a shady area, which requires a change in the f-stop because of the change in the amount of light that is illuminating the actor.

studio Term used to refer to the actual location of the lot, which contains the offices and stages of a major production company; for example, Warner Brothers Studio. It may also indicate the actual building where a particular production is being filmed; for example, studio B. It may also be used to refer to the company that is producing a particular project.

studio zone An area within a given radius of a certain point. Anything outside of that area is considered a distant location. When cast and crew are required to report to a distant location, the production company must compensate them for mileage. If it is far enough away to require that they spend the night, then the production company must provide lodging. In Los Angeles, the studio zone is a 30-mile radius from the corner of La Cienega Boulevard and Beverly Boulevard. See also *mileage.*

sunshade   A small flag or hood that attaches directly to the matte box or the lens to help eliminate any light from striking the lens or the filter. See also *eyebrow; french flag; lens shade.*

Supafrost filter   Trade name of a brand of motion picture camera diffusion filter that is used to soften the overall image. Great care must be taken when using these filters because they are constructed from plastic and scratch very easily. As with other diffusion filters, they come in varying densities and require no exposure compensation.

swish pan   Also called **whip pan.** A very fast camera-panning movement that causes the image to appear blurred. It may be used for a particular dramatic effect or to make a transition between shots or scenes.

sync   A term usually used to indicate a film or scene that is shot with sound and picture being recorded simultaneously.

sync slate   Slate used for identifying all shots done with sound. Attached to it are two hinged pieces of wood, the clap sticks, that are clapped together at the beginning of each sound take (Figure S.10). During editing, the editor matches the film frame that shows the clap sticks striking with the point on the sound track that contains the sound of them striking so that the picture will match the sound track when it is projected.

sync speed   The speed that gives motion pictures the appearance of normal motion to the viewer. In the United States, sync speed is 24 frames per second (fps).

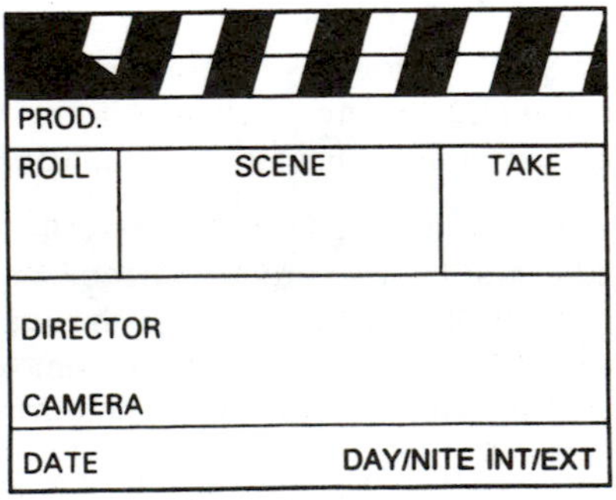

Figure S.10   Sync slate.

T See *total.*

tachometer   A dial or meter, located on the camera, that shows the speed at which the camera is running (Figures F.8, F.9). The 1st AC watches the tachometer during filming to be sure that the camera is maintaining the correct speed.

tail slate   Also called **end slate.** A slate that is photographed at the end of a shot. A tail slate may be needed for a variety of reasons; for example, the camera operator or sound mixer may not have recorded the head slate properly; or it may be a very emotional scene and, in order to not distract the actors, a tail slate is done. When doing a tail slate, the slate is held upside down.

take (take number)   The number that is assigned to a scene each time it is photographed and that refers to a single, uninterrupted shot filmed by the camera. Each time a scene or portion of a scene is shot, it is given a new take number. The director may request many takes of a particular action until he is satisfied with the performance or the action. When the film is developed and processed, selected takes are printed to be used when editing the film.

take-up side   The side of the magazine that contains the exposed film. The unexposed film travels from the feed side of the magazine, through the camera, and then into the take-up side of the magazine (Figures C.11, D.8).

tape measure   A device used by the 1st AC to measure the distance from the film plane of the camera to the subject. This measurement allows the 1st AC to maintain the focus during filming. During each shooting day, the assistant will take many measurements for each scene and for each position that the actor may be in during the shot. The typical tape measure is 50 feet in length and is made of cloth or fiberglass material. For safety reasons, it should not be made of metal.

technicolor 3-strip   An early filming process, introduced in 1932, that used three separate negatives in the camera. Each was sensitive to a different primary color (red, green, blue). During developing and printing in the lab, the three images were combined onto one piece of film to form a color print.

telephoto lens   A lens of long focal length that allows photographing close shots of faraway objects. It has a small angle of view (Figure T.1). A telephoto lens has a tendency to flatten images and reduce perspective. It can make objects appear closer together than they actually are and greatly reduces depth of field.

35mm   The standard film gauge, introduced in 1889, that is used for most professional theatrical and television productions. It is used primarily for larger productions because of its excellent image quality. It may also be used for commercials, music videos, and smaller productions in order to have the highest quality image. The 35mm film stock contains 16 frames per foot and 4 perforations per frame on each side of the film. At normal sync speed of 24 fps, it travels through the camera at the rate of 90 feet per minute.

Figure T.1   Illustration showing the angle of view for a telephoto lens.

three-inch lens (3-inch lens)   A slang term used in the early days of filmmaking to indicate a 75mm lens. The term is still used today by some cameramen.

Tiffen   Trade name of a brand of motion picture camera filters.

tight shot   Similar to a close-up shot, a shot in which the subject being photographed fills the entire frame. It may also be called an extreme close-up. See also *extreme close-up.*

tilt   The vertical, or up-and-down, movement of the camera. By turning the tilt wheel of the geared head or by moving the handle of the fluid head up or down, the camera operator is able to follow any vertical movement of the actor in the scene.

tilt plate   An accessory that is attached between the camera and the head and is used when doing extreme tilt angles with the camera (Figure T.2). It allows the camera operator to tilt the camera at a much steeper angle than is possible with the standard geared head or fluid head. Many geared heads contain a built-in tilt plate for these types of shots.

timed print   A film work print that has been examined and color corrected for each shot. This type of work print is more expensive than a one-light print and is rarely asked for by the production company.

torque motor   A motor on the film magazine that helps to wind the film onto the take-up side during filming. Without this motor pulling the film onto the take-up side, the film would have nowhere to go after running through the camera and would become backed up and jammed in the camera movement. Most of the newer film magazines have a built in torque motor.

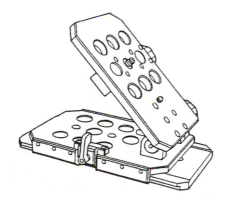

Figure T.2   Tilt plate. (Courtesy of Panavision, Inc.)

total (T) A section on the camera report and also on the film inventory form that indicates the combined total of all good, no-good, and waste footage.

tracking (lens) The ability of a zoom lens to stay centered on a particular point throughout the range of its zoom. The tracking of a zoom lens can be checked by lining up the cross hairs of the ground glass on a point and watching to see if the cross hairs stay centered on the point while slowly zooming the lens in and out. The pan and tilt of the head should be locked so that the camera does not move. If the cross hairs shift either left or right, then the tracking of the lens is off and must be checked by a lens technician.

tracking shot Any shot that has the camera mounted on some type of moving device, such as a dolly or camera car, so that it may follow the action of the actors in the scene.

trailer A very short synopsis of a film, shown to audiences in order to create interest and make them want to see the entire film. They are usually one or two minutes in length and are frequently shown in theaters in groups of three or four prior to the showing of a major film. The trailer usually contains many of the most exciting scenes from a movie, edited in such a way to tease audiences.

triangle See *spreader*.

tripod (also called legs) A three-legged camera support that can be adjusted in height (Figures B1, F.4). Tripods are usually made of wood or metal. A tripod must have a top casting piece that is compatible with the head that will be used for filming. A tripod with a flat base will not accept a head with a bowl base, without some type of adaptor piece. See also *baby legs; standard legs.*

t-stop A number that is similar to the f-stop, but is much more precise (Figure F.12). It indicates the exact amount of light transmitted through the lens. The f-stop indicates the amount of light entering the lens without taking into account light loss due to absorption. The standard series of t-stop numbers is 1, 1.4, 2, 2.8, 4, 5.6, 8, 11, 16, 22, 32, 45, 64, and so on.

tungsten Any light source with a color temperature of approximately 3200 degrees Kelvin. Most film stocks are given an exposure rating for use in both tungsten light and daylight.

turnaround The minimum amount of time that a member of the cast or crew must be given between work shifts, that is, between leaving work on one day and returning the next day. On a union production, the turnaround for the members of the camera department is as follows:

director of photography and camera operator—11 hours, first camera assistant and second camera assistant—9 hours. If turnaround is not observed, the production company must pay the cast or crew member a specified sum of money to compensate them.

turret   A rotating lens mount attached to the front of the camera. More than one lens can be mounted, and the lens for filming can be chosen by rotating the turret. The turret was common on earlier cameras but is no longer used on modern film cameras.

two-inch lens (2-inch lens)   A slang term used in the early days of filmmaking to indicate a 50mm lens. The term is still used today by some cameramen.

two shot   A shot that shows only two people within the frame lines. It may be a close-up, a medium shot, a wide shot, and so on, as long as it only shows two people in the frame.

two Ts   A shot framed so that the top frame line is just above the head and the bottom frame line is just at the breast line of the actor or actress.

Ultracam Trade name for a brand of professional 35mm camera manufactured by Leonetti Company.

undercrank To operate the camera at any speed that is slower than normal sync sound speed of 24 fps. When the final film is projected, it gives the illusion of faster speed on the screen. It is often used in comedy films for a specific effect. As with the term *overcrank*, it originated in the early days of filmmaking when all cameras were cranked by hand.

underexpose Exposing the film to less light than for a normal exposure. Too little light results in a very dark image; for example, in a night scene, if the desired effect is for the actor in the scene to have the correct amount of light shining on him while the background appears slightly darker, then the shot would be underexposed. In general, it is not a good idea to underexpose any shot because it is much harder to correct it in the lab during processing.

union A labor organization that sets the working conditions, wages, hours, and so on, of its members. Most working actors, actresses, and film technicians are members of some type of union. Some of the unions are AFTRA, DGA, IATSE, NABET, and SAG. Many unions also offer some type of benefits to its members, including medical, dental, and pension plans. See also *American Federation of Television and Radio Artists; Directors Guild of America; International Alliance of Theatrical and Stage Employees; National Alliance of Broadcast Employees and Technicians; Screen Actors Guild.*

variable shutter A camera shutter that allows changing the angle for specific filming situations. It allows making longer or shorter exposures while the speed of the camera remains constant. It may be used to make fades and dissolves within the camera. It may also be used by the director of photography to control the exposure and change the depth of field of a shot without changing the exposure setting on the lens. On some cameras containing variable shutters, the shutter angle can be adjusted while the camera is running.

variable-speed camera motor A motor that allows changing the speed of the camera for certain types of shots. It enables filming at very slow speeds or very fast speeds, depending on the desired effect. Many variable-speed camera motors are not crystal sync, and shooting at any speed other than the normal 24 fps is usually done without sound.

video assist A system that incorporates a video camera into the film camera, which allows scenes to be viewed on a monitor or taped on a video recorder as they are shot (Figure M.9). The image striking the mirror shutter of the camera is split so that part of it goes to the viewfinder and part goes to the video camera. This allows the director to see the shot on the video monitor as it is being filmed and also to review the shot by looking at the videotape. It is very helpful for the director to determine if the performance and action were acceptable before moving on to the next shot.

video cables Also called **bnc cables**; **coaxial cables**. Any cables needed to connect the video tap to the video monitor or recorder. They may connect the video tap to the monitor or the monitor to the video recorder (Figure M.9).

video monitor A television monitor that is used along with the video tap to allow the director to view the shot during filming (Figure M.9). See also *video assist*.

video tap   A video camera that is attached to the film camera during shooting. It is used by the director to view the shot on the video monitor as it is being filmed. The image entering the lens is split so that part of it goes to the video camera and is sent by cable to the video monitor. See also *video assist.*

viewfinder   The attachment on the camera that allows the camera operator to view the action (Figures E.3, E.4). During the early days of filmmaking, one type of viewfinder allowed the operator to view the shot through the piece of film. When the antihalation backing was added to the film stock, this system was no longer possible. The next type of viewfinder was called the *rackover viewfinder.* This allowed the entire camera to move independently of the lens so that the lens and viewfinder could be aligned for setting up the shot. It was a good idea for lining up and framing the shot, but the camera operator could not view the shot during filming because the lens had to be repositioned so that it was aligned with the film. Today's modern film cameras all have what is called a *reflex viewfinder.* This allows the camera operator to line up the shot and view it during filming exactly as it will appear on film. The image coming through the lens is reflected onto a mirror shutter and is formed on a ground glass, which is seen through the viewfinder by the camera operator. The ground glass allows the operator to focus the image properly. See also *eyepiece.*

vignetting   Term used to indicate that a portion of the matte box or lens shade is visible or blocking the frame when viewing through the lens. It usually occurs on a very wide angle lens. When looking through the viewfinder, the operator should look around all of the edges of the frame to be sure that nothing is creeping in or blocking any of the frame. In most cases, all that is needed to correct this problem is to slide the matte box back or remove the lens shade so that it is no longer visible through the viewfinder.

Vinten   Trade name of a brand of fluid camera head.

Vitesse geared head   Trade name of a brand of motion picture geared head.

voiceover   Any dialogue or narration that is spoken by a character who is not seen on screen at the time the voice is heard.

w   See *waste*.

waste (W)   The amount of footage remaining on a roll; the film leftover after the good and no-good footage has been totaled. It is too small to be called a *short end* and may be used as a dummy load. In 16mm, waste is usually any roll less than 40 feet, and, in 35mm, it is any roll less than 100 feet. It is written in a section of the camera report and also on the film-inventory report form.

Weaver Steadman   The trade name of a brand of fluid head used in the motion picture industry.

whip   Also called **focus whip**. A slang term used for a type of follow-focus extension. It is called a *whip* because it usually consists of a small round knob attached to a long flexible cable, which connects to the follow-focus mechanism on the camera (Figure W.1).

whip pan   See *swish pan*.

wide-angle lens   A lens that has a very short focal length, or a focal length less than that of a normal lens, and covers a large angle of view (Figure W.2). It may exaggerate perspective. A wide-angle lens is most often

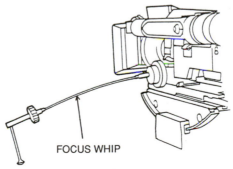

FOCUS WHIP

Figure W.1   Focus whip extension. (Courtesy of Panavision, Inc.)

Figure W.2   Illustration showing angle of view for a wide-angle lens.

used for an establishing or a long shot but may be used for a close-up if the intent is to have a distorted image. When using a wide-angle lens, depth of field is greatly increased.

wide shot   Any shot that encompasses a large field of view. It is usually done a great distance from the subject. A wide shot may also be called an *establishing shot* and is usually done with a wide-angle lens (Figure W.2).

wigwag light   The red warning light that is located outside the door of a sound stage. Whenever this light is illuminated and flashing, it is an indication that filming is going on, and people should be quiet and not enter the stage until the light is turned off. The control for this light is usually kept by the sound mixer who turns it on and off for each shot.

work print   The first print that is made from the edited dailies and that is used by the editor as a working copy during the editing process. This print consists of selected takes from the dailies, which are spliced together in the proper order to form the story. The work print goes through many stages from the first edited version, called a *rough cut,* to the final version, called a *fine cut.* The fine cut of the work print is usually used as a guide when cutting and editing the original negative together. The release print of the film is then made from this edited negative.

wrap   The period at the end of a day's shooting or at the completion of the film or production when all of the equipment is packed away. At the conclusion of an entire filming, the wrap usually consists of cleaning and packing the equipment and returning it to the rental house.

wratten filter (wratten gel)   An optically correct gel filter that is used on a camera lens in place of or in addition to a glass filter. In most cases, the gel filter is placed behind the lens in a special gel-filter holder. These gels are different than the gels used on lights because they are manufactured by Eastman Kodak to very high standards for use on photographic lenses. The standard size of a wratten gel is a 3-inch square.

Zeiss Trade name of a brand of professional motion picture camera lenses.

zoom The effect achieved by turning the barrel of the zoom lens, to change the focal length of the lens, so that the object in the frame appears to move either closer or farther from the camera. When the subject appears to get closer to the camera, it is called *zooming in*, and when the subject appears to move away from the camera, it is called *zooming out*. Zooming in makes the subject become larger and decreases depth of field. Zooming out causes the subject to become smaller and increases depth of field. Doing a zoom move with the lens is not the same as dollying with the camera without changing the lens focal length. When doing a zoom move, the relationship between objects in the frame remains the same.

zoom in The act of changing the focal length of the lens so the angle of view decreases and the focal length of the lens increases. By doing this, the subject becomes larger in the frame. Zooming in decreases depth of field. See also *zoom*.

zoom lens A lens that has varying focal lengths. The focal length is changed by turning an adjustment ring on the barrel of the lens. An object can be held in focus while the angle of view and size of the object are changed during the shot. One advantage of the zoom lens is that it eliminates the need to put a new lens on the camera each time a new focal length is needed. A disadvantage of using a zoom lens instead of a prime lens is that the image quality will not be as good. Because of the many different glass elements contained in a zoom lens, the amount of light reaching the film is reduced a small amount. See also *zoom*.

zoom motor A motor that attaches to the zoom lens to facilitate a smooth zoom move during a shot. It may be built into the lens or it may be an item that you must attach to the lens (Figure Z.1).

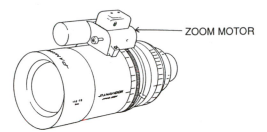

ZOOM MOTOR

Figure Z.1 Zoom lens with zoom motor attached. (Courtesy of Panavision, Inc.)

zoom out The act of changing the focal length of the lens so the angle of view increases and the focal length of the lens decreases. By doing this, the subject becomes smaller in the frame. Zooming out increases depth of field. See also *zoom*.